Instant Pot Cookbook

Over 100 Instant Pot Recipes for The Everyday Home – Simple and Delicious Electric Pressure Cooker Recipes Made for Your Instant Pot

Disclaimer

Remember that the recipes and information in this book are provided for educational purposes only. Everyone has different likes, dislikes, needs and wants and your own cooking should reflect that. The recipes and methods used in this book reflect what has worked for me, the author. Use your own judgment when creating or tweaking the recipes and please exercise caution when opening the lid of your Instant Pot.

Please Bear in mind that eating raw or undercooked food may increase your risk of food-borne illness, so please check that your foods are properly cooked through before eating. Children, the elderly and anyone with a weakened immune system are especially at risk. The use of a cooking thermometer, metal skewer and other tools are highly recommended.

Neither the publisher nor the author takes any responsibility for any possible consequences of reading this book or enjoying the recipes in this book.

Copyright © 2017 Shauna Leroy

Table of Contents

Introduction

Have you noticed the hype in the media about Instant Pots? Everyone from bloggers, to top chefs to regular girls and guys like you and I are raving about how brilliant it is.

All of this will either have you reaching for your credit card and heading out to invest in one of your own RIGHT NOW, or it gets you believing that this is just another one of those pieces of kitchen equipment that will only end up gathering dust in your pantry.

Because surely an Instant Pot can't be THAT brilliant, can it?

Well, actually, **it can.** In fact, I'd go so far as to say that my Instant Pot has completely changed my life.

I know how that sounds because I didn't really believe what I heard in the beginning. Would it *really* cut my time in the kitchen? Would it *really* make my life so much easier?

But I was wrong to have worried. Because I can happily confirm that Instant Pots are awesome.

Thanks to your Instant Pot, you won't have to keep compromising your values as you are serving up junk food to the family yet another time because you don't have time to make healthy food from scratch. You don't have to worry about giving them processed foods with their additives, preservatives, and goodness knows what else lurking inside just because you couldn't face using that scary pressure cooker. You don't have to give them cheap ready-meals because that's all you can afford.

With an Instant Pot, you can make healthy food from scratch, just like your mother used to make in the shortest amount of time imaginable. Amazing!

What is an Instant Pot?

An Instant Pot is a multi-functional counter-top cooker that is simply amazing! Rolled into just one kitchen appliance you have an electric pressure cooker, a slow cooker, a rice cooker, a steamer, a sauté pan, a yoghurt maker and a warming pot too.

It will allow you to start making steel-cut oats overnight so you can wake up to a house smelling heavenly and a well-fed tummy, or rich satisfying soups and stews that will keep you warm all winter, or generous roast meats that flake off the bone, or indulgent desserts that are ready in a fraction of the normal time, amazing vegetarian and vegan meals, fish dishes that are light and fragrant and even fresh homemade yogurts!

I've said it before and I'll say it again- this kitchen appliance will change your life!

A few notes before we get started- I've tried to keep things as straightforward as possible throughout this book and kept exotic ingredients at a minimum. Wherever a recipe requires a less-commonly found food, I'll give an easy substitute you can use instead and still retain all the taste.

Before we get started with the recipes, I'd like to explain more about the benefits of the Instant Pot so you can see why they're so amazing, then I'll walk you through the buttons you'll find on your Instant Pot so you can hit the ground running. Finally, I'll share with you more than 100 recipes that will make your mouth water! These include breakfasts, entrees and appetizers, soups and stews, meat, fish, seafood, poultry, vegetarian and vegan dishes, and then give you many scrumptious desserts that will round off the book nicely.

If you're ready, let's get started.

Chapter 1: What are the Benefits of Using an Instant Pot?

Almost every food blogger, top chef and home cook has been raving about these ingenious pieces of kitchen equipment since they were first launched onto the market a few years back, and they are every bit as good as they say. Instant Pots rock!

To be honest with you, I can't really remember what I did before my Instant Pot came along- these days I do most of my cooking using mine, saving on time, on washing up and on general kitchen mess and fuss.

So why are they so good, exactly? What do Instant Pots offer that regular pressure cookers and other equipment don't? Let me explain...

#1: You'll save tons of time

The best benefit of using an Instant Pot has to be the time it saves you in the kitchen. As I'm sure you'll agree, most of us are pretty busy these days and we don't want to be slaving away for hours over a meal when we could be getting stuff done.

According to the manufacturers, using an Instant Pot will save you a massive 70% of your time in the kitchen. Just think about that for a second...that's quite a saving which comes in handy when you're cooking roast meats, beans, lentils and other foods, which usually take ages.

#2: You'll save money

It's not just time that you'll save when you use an Instant Pot- you'll also save plenty of money on your food and fuel bills.

As the Instant Pot is a sealed device, none of the cooking water can evaporate and instead will stay right inside, leaving your food succulent, delicious, and cook much faster. This means you'll use less energy, which will slash the price of your fuel bill. Brilliant!

And because you can cook healthier foods faster in an Instant Pot, you're more likely to cook from scratch more often and make healthier food choices too. This will reduce your food bills even more!

#3: Your food will be more nutritious

When you boil veggies, much of the nutrition is often lost in the water so you end up eating something slightly limp and much lower in vitamins and minerals than it should be. Not so with the Instant Pot- it allows you to steam your veggies whilst retaining the water, meaning all that nutrition stays right there in your food.

#4: You'll eliminate bacteria and other micro-organisms

Instant Pots cook your food well over boiling point, so you'll kill any nasty bacteria, viruses and other toxins that might be lurking in your food. This is especially important in the case of rice, wheat, corn and beans, as all these foods can harbor toxins, which can make you very sick, and have even been linked to liver cancer.

#5: You'll need less kitchen equipment

You don't need tons of different devices to cook all the food your heart desires- your Instant Pot can do almost everything. This means you can have a cleaner, tidier kitchen and have less to wash up when you're done cooking and more time to do the things you love.

#6: It's much safer than a pressure cooker

Whilst I have tried to use a regular stove-top pressure cooker in the past, I've always been slightly worried that it will explode all over me. But I don't need to worry with the Instant Pot as it has many safety-regulating features that monitor the temperature and pressure, which means we can stay safer. Of course, we're still talking about steam and pressure, so you still need to be careful.

For these reasons Instant Pots are an absolute lifesaver in the kitchen, especially if you have a family, special dietary needs, or you just want to simplify your life without compromising on nutrition or taste. You'll discover for yourself once you start cooking in yours.

But before we dive into the recipes, I'd like to help you get to know your new best (kitchen) friend and explain what all the buttons are about, plus give you some tips on what to expect from your Instant Pot. Sound good? Then let's get to it!

Chapter 2: Making Sense of Those Buttons

As you might have noticed if you're lucky enough to own an Instant Pot already, there are *tons* of buttons on the side, which can seem confusing and overwhelming at first. So, let me reassure you that it's all easy when you know how. In this chapter I'm going to run through all of them in turn, so you can get to grips with using your Instant Pot right away. It's easier than you think!

The main functions

Sauté
Use this to sauté onions, garlic, vegetables and meat in the same way you would on a stove. You can also simmer using this setting by reducing the heat (press the adjust button and set to 'less') or brown by increasing the heat (press the adjust button and set to 'more').

Keep Warm/Cancel Button
It does what it says on the tin! Use it to cancel a function or to keep a dish warm. On some models, you can increase and decrease the temperature.

Manual/Pressure cook button
This is the magic button that will help you pressure cook your dishes for as long as you want. Just use the + and - buttons to adjust the cooking time.

Slow cooker
This will give you a 4-hour cooking time. Just use the + and - buttons to adjust the cooking time as required.

Pressure
This button allows you to switch between high and low pressure.

Yogurt
Use this for making yogurt!

Timer

You can delay the start of cooking by using this handy button. First select the cooking function, adjust as required then press the timer button. You can control the timer by using the + and - buttons.

Pre-set buttons:

Soup

This setting will cook on high pressure for 30 minutes. Use the + and - buttons to adjust the cooking time if required.

Meat/stew

This setting will cook on high pressure for 35 minutes. Use the + and - buttons to adjust the cooking time if required.

Bean/chili

This setting will cook on high for 30 minutes. Use the + and - buttons to adjust the cooking time if required.

Poultry

This setting will cook on high for 15 minutes. Use the + and - buttons to adjust the cooking time if required.

Rice

This setting is fully automatic and will cook your rice on low pressure for as long as it takes.

Multi-grain

This setting will cook on high pressure for 40 minutes. Use the + and - buttons to adjust the cooking time if required.

Porridge

This setting will cook on high pressure for 20 minutes. Use the + and - buttons to adjust the cooking time if required.

Steam

This setting will cook on high for 10 minutes. Use the + and - buttons to adjust the cooking time if required. You will need to use this with the rack or steamer basket for best results.

Cake

Not all models have a cake button, so if you do count yourself lucky! You can select 'less', 'normal' and 'more' to make a variety of sweet treats.

Egg

Some new models also have a special egg setting. Select 'less' for soft-boiled eggs and 'more' for hard-boiled eggs.

Sterilize

You can even sterilize utensils and jars in some models, as well as do some canning. Bear in mind that this isn't possible with all models.

You can usually adjust the time required for all these settings.

I understand that if you've never used an Instant Pot before, that might seem like a massive list there, but don't be put off. I recommend that you get started gently by cooking something easy such as a soup or a stew, then branch out into other dishes and settings. You'll be amazed how quickly it all comes together, and you can make sense of what you're doing.

With all that out of the way, it's time for us to take a leap into the wonderful world of Instant Pot cooking. Are you ready to change your life? (*and that's no exaggeration, either. My Instant Pot certainly changed mine!*)

Chapter 3: The Instant Pot Recipes

Breakfasts

Vanilla Latte Steel-Cut Oats

Don't just start the day with a wholesome and filling bowl of oatmeal! Take it to the next level with this espresso-infused, creamy bowl of awesome. It will keep you warm inside, keep your tummy happy until lunchtime, and keep you coming back for more.

Serves: 2-4

Ingredients:
- 2 ½ cups (590ml) water
- 1 cup (235ml) milk
- 1 cup (90g) steel cut oats
- 2 tbsp. sugar
- 1 tsp. espresso powder
- 2 tsp. vanilla extract
- ¼ tsp. salt

To serve...
- Freshly whipped cream
- Finely grated chocolate

Method:
1. Place the water, milk, oats, sugar, espresso powder, vanilla extract and salt in your Instant Pot.
2. Stir well to dissolve the espresso powder and pop the lid on top.
3. Set to slow cooker function and leave to cook for 6-7 hours.
4. In the morning, remove the lid, stir through any liquid that has separated then pour into bowls.
5. Top with freshly whipped cream and grated chocolate, and enjoy!

Chocolate Cherry Oatmeal

It's YOUR oatmeal, so if you want to lovingly stir through cocoa powder and sprinkle it with chocolate chips, you can, right? After all, they say that oats are good for you.... ;)

Serves: 4

Ingredients:
- 2 cups (180g) oatmeal
- 6 cups (1.4l) water
- 1 cup (235ml) milk
- 2 ½ tbsp. cocoa powder
- 1 tsp. cinnamon
- 1 tsp. vanilla
- 10 oz. (285g) bag frozen cherries

To serve...
- Chocolate chips
- Dried fruit

Method:
1. Place all the ingredients into your Instant Pot and give it all a stir to combine.
2. Then set to slow cooker function and leave for 6-7 hours.
3. In the morning, remove the lid, stir through any liquid that has separated and pour into bowls.
4. Top with chocolate chips (yum!) and a sprinkle of dried fruit.
5. Serve and enjoy!

Berries and Cream Breakfast Cake

Enjoy more breakfast indulgence with this perfectly sweet berry cake. I love the fact you can use whatever you have in your pantry to create a delicious breakfast that's extra-naughty but nice.

Serves: 6

Ingredients:
- 5 free-range eggs
- ¼ cup (50g) sugar
- 2 tbsp. butter, melted
- ¾ cup (185g) ricotta cheese
- ¾ cup (185g) yogurt
- 2 tsp. vanilla extract
- 1 cup (120g) flour
- ½ tsp. salt
- 2 tsp. baking powder
- ½ cup (165g) berry compote or jam
- 1 cup (235ml) water

Method:
1. Start by greasing a Bundt pan with butter then setting to one side.
2. Take a large bowl and mix the eggs and sugar until smooth.
3. Then add the butter, ricotta cheese, yogurt and vanilla and mix until smooth.
4. Now take a separate bowl and combine the flour, salt and baking powder. Stir well to mix.
5. Add the flour to the wet ingredients and stir well, then pour into the pre-prepared tin.
6. Take a spoon and drop spoonful of the berry compote or jam over the mixture in the tin and swirl through with a knife.
7. Now open up your Instant Pot, add the trivet and place the water inside.
8. Lower the cake inside, then cover with the lid, seal and cook on high for 25 minutes.
9. When the timer beeps, allow the pressure to release naturally for 10 minutes then do a quick pressure release.
10. Open the lid, and remove the cake from the Instant Pot and leave to cool slightly.
11. Serve and enjoy!

Baby Breakfast Frittata

Create yourself a breakfast for a king with this power-packed frittata. It's ready in the blink of an eye, and you can throw in whatever your heart desires to take that flavor to the next level and have you ready to face anything the day can throw your way.

Serves: 2-3

Ingredients:
- 5 free-range eggs
- Splash of milk
- Salt and pepper
- Added extras such as cheese, veggies, meats or whatever takes your fancy!

Method:
1. Take a medium bowl and add the eggs, milk and seasonings. Beat well to combine and make it light and fluffy.
2. Then take whatever extras you're using and throw them in to the egg mixture, such as cheese, veggies, sausage, bacon or other meats.
3. Pour the mixture into silicone molds and pop onto the rack in your Instant Pot.
4. Pour 1 cup of water around the silicon then set your Instant Pot to manual high pressure for 5 minutes.
5. Release the steam, remove from the Instant Pot then serve and enjoy!

French Baked Eggs

Baked eggs always feel that extra bit special, especially this simple but delicious version made fast in your Instant Pot. The addition of cheese and meat or fish adds that extra-lovely touch. Enjoy!

Serves: 2-4

Ingredients:
- Olive oil
- 4 slices cheese
- 4 slices meat or small pieces of fish
- 4 free-range eggs
- Fresh herbs, to taste
- Salt and pepper, to taste

Method:
1. Grab four ramekins and rub a small amount of olive oil into the bottom of each, followed by a slice of meat or fish, then cheese.
2. Next break an egg into each ramekin, then fresh herbs or whatever else you desire. (I love fresh chili peppers!)
3. Place them into the steamer basket of your Instant Pot, add water at the bottom of the Instant Pot, and then lower the basket inside.
4. Set your Instant Pot to low pressure for 4 minutes.
5. Release the steam, remove from the Instant Pot then serve and enjoy!

Spicy Mexican Egg Casserole

I'm a big fan of spicy food, whatever time of the day it might be, so I LOVE this Mexican Egg Casserole. It's brilliant for those times when you have a large crowd over, want to create a brunch with a 'wow' factor, or want to give your taste buds an awesome wake-up call!

Ingredients:

- Olive oil
- ½ large red onion, chopped
- 1 clove garlic, chopped
- 1 lb. (450g) mild ground sausage
- ½ cup (60g) flour
- 8 free-range eggs, well-beaten
- 1 red bell pepper, chopped
- 1 can black beans, rinsed
- ½ cup (75g) green onions
- 1 cup (125g) Cotija cheese
- 1 cup (125g) mozzarella cheese

To serve...

- Sour cream
- Cilantro

Method:

1. Turn your Instant Pot onto sauté setting, add a drop of oil then add the onion and garlic, cook until soft and stir often.
2. Add ground sausage to the pot and cook until browned.
3. Take a bowl and add the flour and eggs then stir until combined. Pour this into the Instant Pot, on top of the sausage and onions.
4. Top with the chopped bell pepper, beans, green onion, and cheese, then place the lid on top and lock into place.
5. Set your Instant Pot to high pressure for 20 minutes.
6. Release the steam, then remove the casserole from the Instant Pot then pop onto a plate.
7. Serve with sour cream and cilantro plus as much chili sauce as your heart desires.

Eggs Papin

Yes, even those fancy French breakfast dishes can be yours now you own an Instant Pot, including as this amazing dish. It's ready fast, it's full of protein and antioxidants and will give you that energy boost you need.

Serves: 1-2

Ingredients:
- 2 bell peppers, ends cut off
- 2 free-range eggs, refrigerated
- 2 slices whole wheat bread, toasted
- 2 slices mozzarella or gouda
- 1 small bunch arugula (rocket)

For the Mock Hollandaise sauce...
- ⅔ cup (150g) mayonnaise
- 1 ½ tsp. Dijon mustard
- 3 tbsp. orange juice
- 1 tsp. fresh lemon juice
- 1 tbsp. white wine vinegar
- ½ tsp. salt
- 1 tsp. turmeric

Method
1. Start by making the mock Hollandaise sauce. Place all the sauce ingredients into a bowl and whisk together until smooth. Pop into the fridge to store if needed.
2. Now let's sort those veggies. Cut the ends off the peppers then break an egg inside each.
3. Cover with tin foil and lower into the steamer backer or your Instant Pot with a cup of water.
4. Cover with the lid and lock into place.
5. Cook on low pressure for 3-4 minutes, release the steam and remove from the Instant Pot.
6. Grab a plate and place the toast, followed by the cheese on top, then the arugula, and finally the pepper cups topped with a nice drop of the mock Hollandaise sauce.
7. Enjoy!

Crust-Free Breakfast Quiche

We've popped this recipe under 'breakfast' but honestly, you could enjoy it any time of day. It's quite a filling dish so it's best made when you want to have a lazy day at home reading the papers, and cuddling your nearest and dearest...

Serves: 4-6

Ingredients:
- Olive oil
- 6 large free-range eggs, well beaten
- ½ cup (120ml) half and half (half milk and cream)
- 1/8 tsp. Himalayan salt
- 1/8 tsp. ground black pepper
- 6 oz. (170g) bacon
- ½ cup (90g) diced bell peppers
- 3-4 spring onions, sliced in thin coins, reserving tops for garnish
- ¾ cup (95g) shredded cheese

For the pot...
- 1 ½ cups (350ml) water

To serve...
- 1/4 cup (31g) shredded cheese to garnish (optional)

Method:
1. Take a soufflé dish and grease it with a touch of olive oil, then pop to one side.
2. Now grab a large bowl and throw in the eggs, milk/cream, salt and pepper. Whisk well to combine.
3. Place the bacon, peppers, onion and cheese into the bottom of your soufflé dish and pour the egg mixture over the top.
4. Place the trivet into the bottom of the Instant Pot, along with 1 ½ cups water, then cover the dish with foil and pop inside.
5. Cover with the lid and lock into place.
6. Cook on high pressure for 30 minutes, then leave it to rest for a further 10 minutes.
7. Release the steam and remove from the Instant Pot.
8. Sprinkle with extra cheese and enjoy!

Instant Pot Yogurt with Fruit

Most people don't realize that they can also make yoghurt in their Instant Pot- even I didn't until a friend asked me why I was still buying expensive artisan yoghurt from the store when I could just make my own. And once I tried it, I was hooked. Not only is it much less expensive, it tastes incredible. Try it- you'll see.

Serves: 6-10 (depending on portion size and appetite!)

Ingredients:
- 1 gallon (3.8 liters) milk
- ½ cup (170g) Greek yogurt
- 2 tbsp. vanilla bean paste
- 1 cup (200g) sugar
- 2 cups (350g) chopped fruit (adjust to taste)

Equipment needed...
- Nut Milk Bags or cloth napkins
- 1-Quart jars
- Food thermometer

Method:
1. Pour the milk into your Instant Pot, pop the lid on top and press the button labeled 'yogurt'. Press 'adjust' until you reach the 'boil' option and allow the milk to warm up. This should take less than a minute.
2. Once this is done, carefully remove from the Instant Pot and put it on your counter.
3. Using the food thermometer, cool your milk to 115°F/46.11°C, then place back into your Instant Pot.
4. Pour in the Greek yogurt and vanilla bean paste and stir well until combined. It's really important to get this right or else your yogurt won't work!
5. Now press the 'yogurt' button again so the timer resets and leave for 8 hours.
6. Once it's done, remove the yogurt from the Instant Pot and strain by pouring through the nut milk bags or cloth napkins.
7. Place into the fridge overnight to chill.
8. Now we can make the fruity syrup. Simply place the fruit into a pan with the sugar and bring to the boil. Cool completely and store into fridge until needed.
9. Serve the yogurt topped with this lovely sauce and enjoy!

Quinoa Blueberry Breakfast Bowl

If you're avoiding gluten or simply want a super-food breakfast to start the day right, give this breakfast bowl a try. It's quick, easy and you can throw whatever extras you like on top and tuck in!

Serves: 2-4

Ingredients:
- 1 ½ cups (280g) white quinoa
- 1 ½ cups (352ml) water
- 1 tbsp. cinnamon powder
- ½ cup rasins
- 1 tbsp. honey
- 1 cup (245g) plain yogurt, plus more for serving
- ¾ cup (90g) grated apple
- 1 cup (235ml) apple juice

To serve...
- Blueberries
- Chopped pistachios
- Honey

Method:
1. Start by washing your quinoa under running water then adding to your Instant Pot with the water, and cinnamon.
2. Lock the lid and cook on high for just one minute. Leave for 10 minutes for the pressure to release naturally, then do a quick pressure release.
3. Place into a large bowl then leave to cool.
4. Next add the raisins, honey, yogurt, apple and apple juice and stir well to combine. Pop into the fridge to rest and allow the flavors to combine.
5. Serve with the yogurt mixture plus the pistachios, blueberries and honey.

Breakfast Cobbler

I love the fact we can eat dessert for breakfast, simply by putting the word 'breakfast' in the title! But seriously, you must try this one. Like the other breakfast recipes, it's fast, tastes brilliant and you can give it your personal touch to make it really REALLY amazing. Serve with cream or ice-cream. Go on- I dare you!

Serves: 2

Ingredients:
- 1 pear, diced
- 1 apple, diced
- 1 plum, diced
- 2 tbsp. honey
- 3 tbsp. coconut oil
- ½ tsp. ground cinnamon
- ¼ cup (4 tbsp.) unsweetened shredded coconut
- ¼ cup (30 g) pecan pieces
- 2 tbsp. sunflower seeds

To garnish...
- Coconut whipped cream (optional)

Method:
1. Start by chopping up your fruit and placing into the bowl of your Instant Pot, or a large soufflé dish.
2. Add the honey, coconut oil and cinnamon, then close the lid and steam for 10 minutes.
3. Quick-release the pressure and remove the lid, then place the fruit into a serving bowl.
4. Now place the coconut, pecans, and sunflower seeds into the remaining liquid and press the Sauté button. Cook for around 5 minutes, stirring often so they don't burn.
5. Serve with cream or yogurt.

Baked Apples

The combined smell of apples baking with light cinnamon really takes me back to my childhood, sat on my grandmother's verandah, waiting for my favorite breakfast in the world. So, as you can imagine, I was very happy to find a fast version I can eat whenever the urge takes me.

Ingredients:
- 6 apples
- 1 cup (235ml) apple juice
- ½ cup (100g) sugar
- 2 tbsp. cinnamon

Method:
1. Start by washing your apples, then carefully removing the cores, then place into the bottom of your Instant Pot.
2. Pour the apple juice over the top, sprinkle with sugar and cinnamon and close the lid, locking into place.
3. Cook for 8 minutes then release the pressure and allow it to cool slightly before serving (these things can be HOT!)
4. Serve with whipped cream or ice cream.

Giant Japanese-Style Pancake

Want a fun breakfast? Try these massive Japanese-style pancakes. They're brilliant, pretty much hands off, and you can serve them with any of your favorite toppings. Enjoy!

Ingredients:
- 2 free-range eggs
- 1 ½ cups (350ml) milk
- 2 cups (240g) flour
- 2 ½ tsp. baking powder
- 2 tbsp. granulated white sugar
- Butter or coconut oil

Method:
1. Take a large mixing bowl and add the eggs and milk. Whisk well to combine.
2. Add the remaining ingredients and whisk well to get rid of any lumps.
3. Open the lid of your Instant Pot and grease the pot with a small amount of butter or coconut oil.
4. Pour the batter into the pot, close the lid and cook on low for 45 minutes.
5. Open the Instant Pot and remove the pan. Loosen the sides of the cake with a spatula and serve.
6. Enjoy with your regular pancake toppings – I love blueberries, maple syrup and homemade yogurt!

Soups

Garden Harvest Soup

Simple is often the best. Just throw in whatever veggies are in season or you have at hand, add some onion and garlic, then you have a flavorful, vitamin-rich soup that will stave off any cold or flu.

Ingredients:
- 6 cups (4.1 liters) bone broth or stock
- 10 cups (1.5kg) mixed veggies, cut into chunks (choose whichever you want!)
- 1 onion, chopped
- 3 cloves garlic
- Handful fresh rosemary
- 1 ½ tsp. sea salt
- Freshly ground black pepper, to taste

Method:
1. This is so easy, it's ridiculous! Simply place the broth, veggies, onion, garlic, rosemary and seasoning into your Instant Pot, then pop on the lid and place into sealing position. You don't want it to lock entirely, just seal nicely.
2. Press the 'soup' button and set for 15 minutes cooking time. Depending on your model, you'll see the pressure building before the timer finally starts.
3. Once cooked, release the pressure and open up the lid. Breathe in that lovely smell!
4. Blend until smooth (with an immersion blender) and then pour into a large bowl.
5. Serve and enjoy!

NOTE: This soup stores *really* well in the fridge for easy lunches or dinner whenever you're short on time.

Cuban Black Bean Soup

This soup is sooo much more delicious than it sounds – it's smooth, creamy and perfectly-flavored to keep the Latin spirit in your soul and keep your appetite satisfied all day long. Enjoy!

Serves: 6

Ingredients:
- Olive oil
- 1 large red onion
- 1 red bell pepper
- 5 garlic cloves, minced
- 1 bay leaf
- 1 tsp. ground cumin
- 2 tsp. dried oregano
- 1 lb. (450g) dried black beans, pre-soaked
- 2 tbsp. extra virgin olive oil
- 1 tsp. black pepper
- 1 ½ tsp. salt
- 2 tbsp. sherry vinegar
- ½ cup (120ml) red wine
- 4 cups (940ml) water

To serve...
- Red bell pepper, chopped
- Chopped tomatoes
- Chopped avocado
- Red onion, finely chopped
- Scallion, minced

Method:
1. Start by placing a small amount of olive oil into the bottom of your Instant Pot, switching onto the sauté setting and adding the onion, bell pepper, garlic, bay leaf, cumin and oregano. Cook for around 5 minutes, until the onions are soft.
2. Add the rest of the ingredients and give it all a nice stir.
3. Place the lid and seal. Cook on low for 15 minutes then allow the pressure to release naturally for 15 minutes.
4. Serve, toped with any of the suggested extras and enjoy!

Italian Chicken Soup

Enjoy Italian chicken soup just the way that mamma used to make! All you need is a chicken, a handful of veggies and some Italian-style love for your food, and you'll create the best chicken soup you've ever tasted!

Ingredients:
- 2-3 lb. (900g-1.3kg) chicken
- 2 carrots, roughly chopped
- 1 celery stalk, roughly chopped
- ¼ turnip, cut in 2" cubes
- 4 cups (940ml) water
- 1 tbsp. Italian seasoning
- 2 whole bay leaves
- 3 cloves of garlic, crushed
- 1 medium onion, sliced
- Salt and pepper, to taste

Method:
1. Simply place the ingredients into your Instant Pot, give it a stir, then close the lid and seal.
2. Use the soup setting and cook for 25 minutes.
3. When the timer goes off, release the pressure, remove the chicken and debone the meat.
4. Pop the meat back into the pot and stir well.
5. Partially blend with an immersion blender if preferred, add salt and pepper to taste, then serve and enjoy!

Tomato Basil Soup

Honestly, I was never a fan of tomato soups… until, that is, I tried this fresh, well-rounded version. Balanced, nutritious and delicious, you'll get plenty of vitamin C, and a taste of the summer sun!

Ingredients:
- 1 tbsp. olive oil
- 1 small onion, diced
- 1 small can tomato paste
- 3 x 15 oz. (3 x 425g) cans diced tomatoes
- 2 cups (470ml) chicken stock
- 1 tsp. garlic salt
- 1 tbsp. basil
- 2 tsp. parsley
- 1 tbsp. balsamic vinegar
- ¼ cup (4 tablespoons) sugar

Method:
1. Place the olive oil into the bottom of your Instant Pot, then turn on the sauté setting.
2. Add the onion and tomato paste. Cook for around 5 minutes until the onion goes nice and soft.
3. Next add the tomatoes, stock, garlic salt, basil and parsley and give it all a nice stir.
4. Pop the lid on, seal and switch on the soup setting. Cook for 10 minutes.
5. When the alarm goes off, allow it to sit for 10 minutes before releasing the pressure.
6. Open up then stir through the vinegar and sugar.
7. Blend well with your immersion blender, then serve and enjoy.

Fresh Corn Chowder

Who doesn't love fresh corn chowder for lunch or dinner? You've got those succulent corn pieces, that melt-in-the-mouth potato and that flavorsome bacon which warms your soul from the inside. This makes enough for a whole family, or to store in the fridge for a delicious week of lunch.

Serves: 6-8

Ingredients:
- 6 ears fresh corn
- 4 tbsp. butter
- ½ cup (75g) chopped onion
- 3 cups (705ml) water
- 2 medium potatoes, diced
- 2 tbsp. corn starch
- 2 tbsp. water
- 3 cups (705ml) half-and-half or milk
- 1 /8 tsp. cayenne pepper
- 4 slices bacon, cooked and diced
- 2 tbsp. fresh parsley
- Salt and pepper, to taste

Method:
1. Start by cutting that corn off the kernel with a nice sharp knife, then set to one side.
2. Now place the butter into your Instant Pot, turn onto sauté, add the onions and cook for around 5 minutes until the onion softens.
3. Next add the water and the corn then replace the lid, locking into place.
4. Select high pressure and pop the timer on for 10 minutes. When the timer is off, release pressure.
5. Using a slotted spoon, remove the corn from the broth but leave the liquid in the pot.
6. Next place the steamer basket inside, add the potatoes followed by the corn and lock that lid on.
7. Cook on high pressure for 4 minutes. When timer sounds, do a quick pressure release, and completely remove the steamer basket containing those veggies.
8. Now take a small bowl and dissolve the corn starch in 2 tablespoons of water. Pour into the pot and cook on simmer until the soup thickens.
9. Finally, stir through the milk, cayenne, steamed corn and potatoes, bacon, parsley and seasoning and then gently warm.
10. Serve and enjoy!

Cheddar Broccoli & Potato Soup

Mmmm...cheese and broccoli. How awesome! It tastes wonderful and the broccoli is a superfood, so you get flavor and might even live longer once you've eaten it. Do we need any more excuses? I think not!

Serves: 4-6 servings

Ingredients:
- 2 tbsp. butter
- 2 cloves garlic, crushed
- 1 medium sized broccoli head, broken into large florets
- 2 lbs. (900g) potatoes, peeled and cut into small chunks
- 4 cups (940ml) vegetable broth
- Salt and pepper, to taste
- 1 cup (235ml) half and half
- 1 cup (125g) cheddar cheese, shredded

Method:
1. Place the butter into the bottom of your Instant Pot, turn on the sauté setting and add the garlic, stirring often.
2. Next add the broccoli, potatoes, broth and seasonings, then place the lid on top, seal and cook on high for 5 minutes.
3. Leave for 10 minutes to release naturally, then add the half and half plus the cheese. Stir well and blend with an immersion blender if you like.
4. Adjust with seasoning then serve and enjoy!

Minestrone Soup

This perfect Minestrone soup has everything a soup should contain- veggies, beans, garlic, cheese and al-dente paste to keep you charged and ready for action.

Serves: 2-4

Ingredients:
- 2 tbsp. olive oil
- 1 large onion, diced
- 1 large carrot, diced
- 2 stalks celery, diced
- 3 cloves garlic, minced
- 1 tsp. dried oregano
- 1 tsp. dried basil
- Sea salt and pepper, to taste
- 28 oz. (790g) can San Marzano tomatoes
- 4 cups (940ml) vegetable broth
- 1 bay leaf
- ½ cup (15g) fresh spinach, shredded
- 1 cup (100g) elbow pasta
- 15 oz. (425g) can cannellini beans
- 1/3 cup (50g) finely grated Parmesan cheese

Method:
1. Put the olive oil into the bottom of your Instant Pot, turn on the sauté setting.
2. Add the onion, carrot, celery and garlic. Cook for around 5 minutes until the onion gets nice and soft.
3. Next add the rest of the ingredients (apart from the beans and Parmesan) and give it all a nice stir.
4. Close the lid, seal, then cook on high pressure for 6 minutes.
5. Leave to sit for a minute or two before using a quick pressure release.
6. Stir through the white beans and ladle into bowls.
7. Sprinkle with the Parmesan and enjoy!

Chicken Faux Pho

Ready for something slightly different? I thought so! Try this Asian-inspired chicken soup. You get a mouth full of flavor and feel like you're somewhere exotic on your vacation. Awesome!

Serves: 6-8

Ingredients:
- 1 tbsp. coriander seed
- 4 lbs. (1.8kg) assorted chicken pieces, bone-in and skin on
- 1" (2.2cm) ginger, peeled and roughly chopped
- 1 tsp. green cardamom pods
- 1 black cardamom pod
- 1 cinnamon stick
- 4 garlic cloves
- 1 cup (50g) fresh cilantro
- 2 medium onions, quartered
- 1 lemon grass stalk, trimmed and cut into 2-inch pieces
- ¼ cup (4 tbsp.) fish sauce
- Water, to cover
- Sea salt to taste
- 1 head Bok Choy, roughly chopped
- 1 large daikon root, spiralized

To garnish...
- Lime wedges
- Fresh basil
- Mung bean sprouts
- 2 jalapenos, thinly sliced
- ¼ onion, thinly sliced

Method:
1. Open up your Instant Pot, turn on the sauté setting and add the coriander seeds. Cook for 5 minutes until golden.
2. Now add the chicken pieces, the spices, cilantro, onion, lemon grass and fish sauce, followed by enough water to cover it all.
3. Close the Instant pop, seal and cook on high for 30 minutes.

4. Release the pressure once the timer goes off and remove the chicken. Shred and place to one side.
5. Now strain the broth through a sieve and place back into the Instant Pot, adjusting seasoning if required.
6. Bring to a simmer and add the Bok Choy and daikon noodles. Cook for 5 minutes.
7. Now place the noodles and chicken into generous bowls, top with the broth, add any of the garnishes you fancy from the list, then serve and enjoy!

Carrot & Coconut Soup

Carrot and coconut soup is a classic must-try soup that's suitable for vegans, vegetarians and anyone looking to liven up their life with some veggies. It's ready quickly too, so you can make it anytime, have it on the table fast and tuck right in.

Serves: 4

Ingredients:
- 1 tbsp. unsalted butter
- 1 medium onion
- 1 clove garlic
- 1-piece small ginger
- 1 lb. (450g) carrots
- ¼ tsp. brown sugar
- Kosher salt freshly ground pepper
- 2 cups (470ml) low-sodium chicken broth
- 1 x 13.5 oz. (380ml) can unsweetened coconut milk
- Fresh cilantro & chili sauce, as garnish

Method:
1. Place the butter into the bottom of your Instant Pot, turn on the sauté setting and add the onions. Cook until soft.
2. Then add the garlic and ginger, followed by the carrots, brown sugar and seasonings. Cook for a further 2-3 minutes.
3. Stir through the chicken broth and coconut milk then place the lid on top and seal.
4. Cook on high for 6 minutes and leave to sit for 10 minutes before doing a quick pressure release.
5. Use an immersion blender, season with salt and pepper, and enjoy!

Ham & White Bean Soup

My grandmother used to make a delicious version of this classic soup. Actually, I'll admit it- I stole this recipe from her, but I'm sure she wouldn't mind. Think tender ham, soft veggies, fragrant herbs and a whole lot of flavor. Yum!

Serves: 8

Ingredients:
- 1 tbsp. olive oil
- 1 medium carrot, chopped
- 1 medium onion, chopped
- 3 cloves garlic, minced
- 1 medium tomato, peeled and chopped
- 1 lb. (450g) white beans
- 1 lb. (450g) ham, cubed
- 4 cups (940ml) vegetable stock
- 2 cups (470ml) water
- 2 tsp. salt
- 1 tsp. freshly ground black pepper
- 1 tsp. dried mint
- 1 tsp. thyme
- 1 tsp. paprika

Method:
1. Put olive oil into the bottom of your Instant Pot, turn on the sauté setting and add the carrot, onion, garlic and tomato. Cook 5 minutes, stirring often.
2. Add the remaining ingredients, close the lid and seal.
3. Cook on high for 15 minutes, then leave for 10 minutes to allow the pressure to naturally release, then do a quick release.
4. Open up, ladle into bowls then enjoy!

Lentil and Sausage Soup

This one is most certainly a crowd-pleaser. The combination of sausage, lentils and tomato together really hits the spot and keeps you filling that bowl! All I can say is try it- you'll see.

Serves: 10

Ingredients:
- 1 tbsp. olive oil
- 2 stalks celery, chopped
- 2 carrots, chopped
- ½ onion, chopped
- ½ lb. (225g) sausage, ground
- 3 ½ cups (820ml) beef broth
- 2 tsp. garlic, minced
- 1 cup (200g) lentils rinsed, drained
- 1 x 15 oz. (425g) can diced tomatoes with juices
- 2 cups (60g) spinach
- ½ tsp. salt
- ½ tsp. black pepper

Method:
1. Put the olive oil into the bottom of your Instant Pot, and turn on the sauté setting.
2. Add the celery, carrots and onion. Cook for around 5 minutes until the onion gets nice and soft.
3. Add the crumbled chicken sausage, stir well and cook for 5 minutes.
4. Add the rest of the ingredients, give it a stir then place the lid and seal.
5. Cook on high for 25 minutes.
6. When the timer goes off, do a quick pressure release and stir well.
7. Serve and enjoy!

Curried Butternut Squash Soup

This soup is like pouring the Fall into your bowl and allow it to warm you up from the tips of your toes to the top of your head. The squash helps boost your immune system, the spices keep your taste buds satisfied and the coconut just takes it to a whole new level.

Serves: 4

Ingredients:
For the soup...
- 1 tsp. extra-virgin olive oil
- 1 large onion, chopped
- 2 cloves garlic, minced
- 1 tbsp. curry powder
- 1 x 3 lb (1.6kg) butternut squash, peeled and cubed
- 1 ½ tsp. salt
- 3 cups (705ml) water
- ½ cup (120ml) coconut milk

To serve...
- Hulled pumpkin seeds
- Dried cranberries

Method:
1. Start by opening your Instant Pot, turning onto sauté and adding the olive oil.
2. Add the onion and sauté until soft.
3. Add the garlic and curry powder and cook for another minute.
4. Add the butternut squash, salt and water, then cover with the lid, seal and cook on the soup setting for 30 minutes. If you don't have a soup setting, simply cook on high for 30 minutes.
5. Allow the pressure to release naturally for 10 minutes then do a quick pressure release and carefully open the lid.
6. Use an immersion blender to whizz the soup, then stir through the coconut milk plus any additional seasoning you'd like.
7. Serve and enjoy!

Starters and Side Dishes

Refried Beans

These tasty refried beans are so packed with flavor and they're so easy to make – I love them! You can eat them as a side with your favorite Mexican dishes or do as I do and spread them lovingly on toast.

Serves: lots!

Ingredients:
- 1 ½ cups (225g) chopped onion
- 4-5 garlic cloves, roughly chopped
- 1 jalapeno, seeded and chopped
- 2 tsp. dried oregano
- 1 ½ tsp. ground cumin
- ½ tsp. ground black pepper
- 3 tbsp. lard
- 4 cups (940ml) chicken broth
- 4 cups (940ml) water
- 2 lb. (900g) dried pinto beans, soaked
- 1-2 tsp. sea salt

Method:
1. Open up your Instant Pot and add all the ingredients, except for the beans and the salt.
2. Strain the soaked beans in a colander and then throw into your Instant Pot. Stir well to combine.
3. Place the lid on top, seal and cook for 45 minutes on high. If you have a bean/chili setting on your Instant Pot, use this.
4. Allow to rest to naturally release the pressure, then open the lid.
5. Add salt to taste then blend using an immersion blender.
6. Serve and enjoy!

Sweet and Orangey Brussels Sprouts

Whoever claims they don't like Brussels sprouts will soon change their tune when they sample these deliciously citrus treats. They taste great with your Thanksgiving meal, perfect when friends come over or brilliant when you want to enjoy a nibble with a difference.

Serves: 8

Ingredients:
- 2 lbs. (900g) Brussels sprouts
- ¼ cup (60ml) freshly squeezed orange juice
- 1 tsp. grated orange zest
- 1 tbsp. butter
- 2 tbsp. maple syrup or honey
- ¼ tsp. black pepper, or to taste
- ½ tsp. salt, or to taste

Method:
1. Start by cutting the bottoms off the Brussels sprouts and cut in half if they are large.
2. Place the sprouts into the Instant Pot, along with the rest of the ingredients.
3. Close the lid, seal and cook on high for 3-4 minutes.
4. When the timer has stopped, do a quick pressure release, open the lid and give everything a nice stir.

Parmesan Roasted Potatoes

You just can't go wrong with roasted potatoes, especially these crispy, cheesy ones. They've got that salty crunch, they'll melt in your mouth and they'll take you right to potato heaven! Enjoy!

Serves: 4-8

Ingredients:
- 2 lbs. (900g) baby or fingerling potatoes
- 2-3 tbsp. olive oil
- 2 tbsp. dried minced chives
- 3-4 garlic cloves
- ½ cup (120ml) chicken or vegetable stock
- Salt and pepper, to taste
- 1/3 cup (50g) finely grated Parmesan cheese

Method:
1. Start by taking the potatoes and piercing them with a fork.
2. Put the olive oil into the bottom of your Instant Pot, turn on the sauté setting and add the potatoes, chives and garlic. Cook for around 6 minutes, until browned.
3. Add the stock, stir well and place the lid. Seal.
4. Cook on high for 7 minutes, then let it rest for 10 minutes to allow the pressure to release naturally. Then do a quick pressure release.
5. Toss with Parmesan and seasoning and enjoy!

Macaroni and Cheese

Your days of getting factory-processed mac'n'cheese in a box are most definitely over and done with. Because, for a fraction of the price, time and effort, you can make mouth-watering mac'n'cheese right there in your Instant Pot. Awesome!

Serves: 8

Ingredients:
- 1 lb. (450g) pasta
- 4 cups (940ml) water
- 1 tbsp. dry mustard powder
- 1 tsp. hot sauce
- 2 tbsp. butter
- 1 lb. (450g) cheddar cheese
- 1 cup (125g) Monterey Jack cheese
- 1 cup (235ml) milk or half and half

Method:
1. Place the pasta, water, mustard and hot sauce into your Instant Pot and stir.
2. Close the lid, seal and cook on high for 4 minutes.
3. When the timer beeps, do a quick pressure release and check the pasta. If you need to drain, do so now and pop it back into the pan.
4. Stir through the butter, cheese and milk and let the cheese melt perfectly.
5. Serve and enjoy!

Real Baked Beans

Those baked beans you find in a can are so far removed from the traditional kind- you'll be shocked when you get your teeth around these (but in a good way!). The flavor is complex and will warm your soul!

Serves: 4-6

Ingredients:
- Olive oil
- 1 cup (225g) bacon, diced
- ½ medium onion, diced
- 1 cup (235ml) chicken stock
- 1 tsp. sea salt
- 1 tsp. pepper
- 1 tsp. dry mustard
- 1 tbsp. Worcestershire sauce
- 1 tbsp. balsamic vinegar
- 2 tbsp. tomato paste
- 1/3 cup (65g) dark brown sugar
- 1/3 cup (113g) molasses
- 1 cup (235ml) water
- 2 cups (525g) dry white beans, soaked

Method:
1. Put the olive oil into the bottom of your Instant Pot, turn on the sauté setting and add the bacon. Cook for 2-3 minutes until brown, then take out and dry on kitchen paper.
2. Add the onions to the fat and cook until soft.
3. Pour the chicken stock into the Instant Pot and stir well, then add the remaining ingredients. Drain the beans and add these too.
4. Cook on high for 40 minutes, then quick release and open the lid.
5. Stir through the bacon, then put the lid back on and cook for up to ten more minutes if needed.
6. Serve and enjoy!

Cilantro Lime Rice

Don't settle for average rice – try this lime and cilantro injected beauty instead. It takes just a few minutes and will impress your guests, please your family and even get your date to come back for more...

Serves: 4

Ingredients:
- 1 cup (185g) white rice
- 1 cup (235ml) water
- ½ cup cilantro, chopped
- 3 1/2 tbsp. lime juice
- Pinch of salt

Method:
1. Start by washing the rice under running water until it runs clear.
2. Place into your Instant Pot, followed by the water and give it a good stir.
3. Place the lid, seal and press the 'rice' button. Your Instant Pot knows what to do so just leave it until you hear the beep.
4. Leave the steam to release naturally then open the lid.
5. Stir through the cilantro and lime juice and add a little salt if needed.
6. Serve and enjoy!

Taco Hummus

This hummus isn't your usual hummus. Its ultra-creamy, protein-packed and it's loaded with awesome taco seasoning to wake up your taste buds and fill your tum. I've said that it will serve six, but really, I could eat the whole lot myself!

Serves: 6

Ingredients:
- 1 cup (200g) dried chickpeas, soaked
- 3 cups (705ml) water
- 2 tbsp. olive oil
- 2 tbsp. tahini
- ¼ cup (4 tbsp.) lime juice
- 1 x 1 oz. (22.5g) packet taco seasoning

Method:
1. Drain the garbanzo beans and put into your Instant Pot with the water.
2. Place the lid, seal and cook on high for 70 minutes.
3. Once you hear the timer, use the quick pressure release and open, then drain the liquid away.
4. Place your beans into the food processor with the olive oil, tahini, lime juice and seasoning. Blend until smooth.
5. Pop into the fridge until you're ready to enjoy it!

Creamy, Fluffy Potato Salad

Potato salad is one of those side dishes that sounds like it deserves to stay back in the 80's. Yet whenever anyone serves it up at a BBQ or summer event, you'll hear gasps of delight as they all tuck in. Keep them happy- make your own.

Serves: 8 – 12

Ingredients:
- 2 ½ tsp. salt
- 3 tbsp. apple cider vinegar
- 4 cups (940ml) cold water
- 3 1/3 lbs. (1.5kg) Russet potatoes
- 3 free-range eggs

For the dressing…
- 1 small red onion
- 1 dill pickle or cornichon
- 3 stalks celery
- 8 – 10 stems fresh dill
- 1 cup (250g) full fat mayonnaise
- 1 tbsp. whole grain mustard
- 1 tbsp. apple cider vinegar
- ½ tsp. garlic powder
- Salt and black pepper, to taste

Method:
1. Put salt, vinegar and water into your Instant Pot, followed by the potatoes and the eggs.
2. Close the lid, seal and cook on low for 0 minutes (this might sound weird, but the pressure takes about 20 minutes to reach peak, by which time the eggs and potatoes are cooked.).
3. Immediately release the pressure, then open up.
4. Drain the potatoes, place onto a tray and cover with the vinegar. Leave to cool.
5. Allow the eggs to cool in cold water then chop finely.
6. Next make the salad dressing by combining all the dressing ingredients and stirring well to combine.
7. Season with extra salt and pepper if required, then serve and enjoy!

Chinese Broccoli with Garlic

I've always been a big fan of broccoli (strange, I know!) but I must admit that the addition of garlic, vinegar and salt takes it to a whole new level. You can have this ready in the blink of an eye and tuck into tender, nutrient-packed goodies fast. Yum!

Serves: 2-4

Ingredients
- ½ cup (120ml) water
- 1 large head of broccoli, chopped into florets
- 1 tablespoon olive oil
- 6 garlic cloves, minced
- 1 tablespoon vinegar
- Salt and pepper, to taste

Method
1. Start by pouring ½ cup water into your Instant Pot, and place the steamer basket inside.
2. Place the broccoli florets into the steamer rack, place the lid, seal and cook on low pressure for 0 minutes (see my earlier notes on why this isn't as strange as it sounds!)
3. When the timer sounds, turn off and do a quick pressure release.
4. Take out the broccoli then set aside to air dry.
5. Now remove the water, dry the inner pot and turn on sauté setting.
6. Add the olive oil and sauté the garlic for a few seconds, followed by the broccoli, vinegar, and salt.
7. Stir and allow it to cook for around 5 minutes.
8. Serve and enjoy!

Green Beans with Bacon

These green beans are oh-so minimalist, with just enough bacon to give the dish that texture and bite. Give them a try!

Serves: lots

Ingredients:
- 1 lb. (450g) green beans
- 1 cup (235ml) water
- ¼ cup (55g) bacon bits
- ½ tbsp. butter
- Pinch salt and pepper, to taste

Method:
1. Start by preparing your beans by cutting the ends off and wash them very well.
2. Pour the water into your Instant Pot, and place the steamer basket.
3. Add the bacon and green beans and cook for 5 minutes.
4. When cooked, put into a bowl and top with the butter, and salt and pepper to taste.
5. Serve and enjoy!

Meat

Beef Stew

My mother always used to make a big pan of beef stew whenever the family came to visit because she knew it would keep the conversation flowing and keep those appetites satisfied. And boy, didn't it do the job! You can enjoy the same with this easy beef stew, surrounded with chunks of tasty veggies and taste.

Serves: 6

Ingredients:
- 1 lb. (450g) stewing meat, chopped into chunks
- ½ cup (60g) flour
- 2 tbsp. butter
- 2 cups (470ml) beef stock
- 4 large potatoes, cut in 1-inch chunks
- 1 cup carrots, chopped
- 3 turnips, chopped
- 8 oz. (225g) fresh mushrooms, quartered
- 1 x 14 oz. (450g) bag frozen pearl onions (don't defrost)
- 2 cloves garlic, minced
- 2 tsp. salt
- 1 tsp. dried rosemary
- 1 tsp. dried thyme
- 2 tbsp. tomato paste
- 1 tbsp. Worcestershire sauce
- 1 tbsp. soy sauce
- 2 tsp. brown sugar
- ½ cup (75g) peas

Method:
1. Start by grabbing a nice big bowl, adding the flour followed by the meat then tossing to cover completely.
2. Put the butter in the bottom of your Instant Pot, turn on the sauté setting and add the meat. Cook until it gets brown, stirring often.
3. Now add the stock, veggies, onions, garlic, salt, herbs, tomato paste, Worcestershire sauce, soy sauce and brown sugar and give it a nice stir to combine.
4. Pop the lid on top, and seal then cook on meat/stew setting for 30 minutes.
5. When the timer sounds, allow the pressure to release naturally, then carefully remove the lid.
6. Stir in the peas and then reheat until peas are warm.
7. Serve and enjoy. Tastes brilliant with old-fashioned bread and butter.

Mongolian Beef

With the gentle Asian flavors of ginger, garlic and soy sauce, this beef dish is a winner! It's fast, very yummy and you'll definitely add it to the list of go-to recipes.

Serves 4-6

Ingredients:
- 2 tbsp. olive oil
- 2 lbs. (900g) top sirloin steak, trimmed
- 1 tsp. ginger, minced
- 3 cloves garlic, minced
- ½ cup (120ml) water
- 1 cup (235ml) soy sauce
- 1 ½ cups (300g) dark brown sugar
- 2 tbsp. corn starch
- 3 tbsp. cold water

Method:
1. Put the olive oil in the bottom of your Instant Pot, turn on the sauté setting and add the meat. Cook until browned to perfection then pop onto a place.
2. Now add the ginger and garlic, and cook for a further minute.
3. Stir through the water, soy sauce and brown sugar, stirring to combine well, then add the meat back into the pot.
4. Pop on the lid, seal and cook on high for 12 minutes.
5. When the timer sounds, use a quick pressure release, then carefully open the lid and switch off.
6. Take a small bowl and combine the water and corn starch, stirring well until combined. Slowly add this mixture to the pot until the sauce thickens.
7. Serve and enjoy!

Beef Stroganoff

This beef stroganoff is simply divine. Perhaps it's the sour cream. Perhaps it's the flecks of thyme. Perhaps it's the excitement you'll be feeling as you prepare this creamy, soul-nourishing meal...

Serves: 4-6

Ingredients:
- 2 tbsp. olive oil
- ½ onion, diced
- Salt and freshly ground black pepper, to taste
- 2 lbs. (900g) beef stew meat, chopped
- 3 cloves garlic, minced
- ½ tsp. dried thyme
- 2 tbsp. soy sauce
- 3 cups (225g) chopped mushrooms
- 2 tbsp. all-purpose flour
- 3 cups (705ml) chicken broth
- 1 lb. (450g) package wide egg noodles
- ¾ cup (185ml) sour cream

Method:
1. Put the olive oil in the bottom of your Instant Pot, turn on the sauté setting and add the onion. Cook until perfectly soft (usually around 5 minutes) then stir through the salt and pepper.
2. Take the beef and season with salt and pepper, before adding to the pot. Give everything a nice stir until it's browned on both sides, then add the garlic, thyme and soy sauce, stirring well.
3. Next add the mushrooms and the flour, then stir again, followed by the chicken broth.
4. Pop the lid on top, seal and cook on high for 10 minutes.
5. Once the timer sounds, do a quick pressure release then open the lid carefully.
6. Throw in the egg noodles, put the lid back on, seal then cook on high pressure for 5 minutes.
7. Allow the pressure to release naturally for 5 minutes, then do a quick pressure release.
8. Carefully open the lid, pour in the sour cream and stir well to combine.
9. Serve and enjoy!

Simple Beef Curry

Sometimes you just need to satisfy that craving for curry, and you need to do it fast. That's when this coconut-infused curry will really deliver. It contains the regular ingredients plus potatoes and carrots for that added yum-factor.

Serves 2-4

Ingredients:
- 2 tbsp. olive oil
- 1 onion, chopped
- 5 cloves garlic, minced
- 1 lb. (450g) beef stewing meat, chopped
- 3 large potatoes, chopped into chunks
- 6 carrots, peeled and sliced
- 1 cup (235ml) full fat canned coconut milk
- ½ cup (120ml) bone broth or veggie broth
- 1 ½ tbsp. curry powder
- 1 tsp. sea salt
- ½ tsp. pepper
- 1 tsp. oregano
- ¼ tsp. paprika

Method:
1. Put the olive oil in the bottom of your Instant Pot, turn on the sauté setting and add the onions and garlic, cooking for about 2 minutes until the onion starts to soften.
2. Next add the meat and cook until browned on both sides.
3. Add the remaining ingredients then stir through to ensure everything is combined well.
4. Pop on the lid, seal then cook on the meat/stew setting for 30 minutes.
5. Do a quick pressure-release, open up the lid, and then ladle into bowls.
6. Enjoy with rice or bread. Yum!

Chili Lime Steak Bowl

Yay for the instant Mexican meal! This one just contains steak strips, avocados and spices, but really...do you actually need more?

Serves: 4

Ingredients:
- 1 tbsp. olive oil
- 1 tsp. minced garlic
- 1.5 lbs. (680g) of fajita steak strips, cut into cubes
- 1 tbsp. water
- 2 tsp. lime juice
- ½ tsp. chili powder
- ½ tsp. sea salt
- ½ tsp. cracked pepper
- 1 tsp. Hot Chili sauce
- 2-3 avocadoes, diced

Method:
1. Put the olive oil in the bottom of your Instant Pot, turn on the sauté setting and add the garlic. Cook until brown.
2. Next add the rest of the ingredients, stir well then pop the lid on top.
3. Seal then cook on high for 10 minutes.
4. When the timer sounds, do a quick pressure release and carefully remove the lid.
5. Use a wooden spoon to carefully break the meat into chunks then turn back onto sauté mode.
6. Stir often and allow it to thicken before serving.
7. Enjoy!

Italian Beef Dinner

I've got to admit that the Italians really do the best beef in the world. With tomatoes, garlic, basil and a handful of veggies, you'll be satisfied, energized and feel pretty healthy too. Priceless!

Serves: 4-6

Ingredients:
- Olive oil
- 1 onion, chopped
- 2-3 cloves garlic, chopped
- 3 cups (375g) carrots
- 3 lbs. (1.3kg) small red potatoes
- ¼ cup (60ml) water
- 1 tsp. dried basil
- 15 oz. (425g) can tomato sauce
- 3 lb (1.3 kg) beef chuck roast
- Salt and pepper, to taste
- Pinch paprika, to taste

Method:
1. Put the olive oil in the bottom of your Instant Pot, turn on the sauté setting and add the onion and the garlic. Cook for 2-3 minutes until brown.
2. Next add the carrots and the potatoes, followed by the water, herbs, tomato sauce, beef, and seasonings.
3. Pop on the lid, seal and cook on meat/stew for 45 minutes.
4. Allow the pressure to release naturally then carefully open up.
5. Serve and enjoy!

Tender Braised Short Ribs

Yes, you can even do deliciously sticky ribs in your Instant Pot and have them ready for the crowds to devour. Speaking of crowds, these do great whether you have a gathering at home, or it's just a candlelit dinner for the two of you.

Serves: 4-6

Ingredients:
- 2 lbs. (900g) beef short ribs
- ½ tsp. salt
- ¼ tsp. black pepper
- 1 ½ tsp. olive oil
- 1 ¼ cups onion, diced
- 1 tsp. garlic, minced
- ½ cups (120ml) red wine
- ⅓ cups (75g) ketchup
- 1 ½ tbsp. soy sauce
- 1 tbsp. Worcestershire sauce
- 1 tbsp. brown sugar
- 1 tsp. dried thyme

Method:
1. Sprinkle the ribs with salt and pepper and cut into segments.
2. Switch your Instant Pot onto sauté and add the ribs, searing lightly, then remove.
3. Add olive oil, then the onions and garlic and cook until softened.
4. Pop the ribs into the pot again, followed by the wine, ketchup, soy sauce, Worcestershire sauce and brown sugar. Mix well to combine.
5. Add the thyme then pop the lid on and seal.
6. Cook on meat/stew setting for 35 minutes.
7. Allow the pressure to release naturally for five minutes then do a quick pressure release.
8. Serve and enjoy!

Quick Beef Chili

Although I love chili, I understand that not everyone is such a fan of spice. That's why this recipe is a winner. It's easy, it's fast and it's bursting with beans, tomatoes and much more. Enjoy!

Serves: 2-4

Ingredients:
- Olive oil
- 1 lb. (450g) ground beef
- ¾ tsp. salt
- ½ small onion, chopped
- 1 medium red bell pepper, chopped
- 1 x 15 oz. (425g) can black beans, drained and rinsed
- 1 x 10 oz. (380ml) mild diced tomatoes with green chilies, drained
- ½ cup (120ml) canned tomato sauce
- ¾ cup (180ml) beef broth
- 1 tsp. cumin
- ½ tsp. chili powder
- ½ tsp. paprika
- ¼ tsp. garlic powder
- Black pepper, to taste

Method:
1. Put the olive oil in the bottom of your Instant Pot, then add the beef and cook until brown. Sprinkle over some salt and stir well.
2. Now add the onion and bell pepper, and cook until the veggies start to get a bit soft.
3. Finally add the rest of the ingredients, pop the lid on, seal and cook on high for 20 minutes.
4. Allow the pressure to naturally release then serve.
5. Top with whatever takes your fancy. Why not try chopped red onions, cilantro, lime, sour cream, shredded cheese, avocado and even some extra chili if you like it hot!

Lamb and Sweet Potato Stew

This flavor-rich stew, infused with warming cumin and sweet cinnamon takes me right back to my youth when I was lucky enough to spend time in North Africa. Take a deep breath as it's cooking and picture yourself somewhere tropical.

Serves: 2-4

Ingredients:
- 1 ½ tsp. salt
- ½ tsp. black pepper
- 1 tsp. cumin
- 2 tsp. ground coriander
- 1 ½ lb. (680 g) lamb shoulder, cut into 2-inch (5 cm) pieces
-
- 1 tbsp. olive oil
- 1 onion, roughly chopped
- 4 garlic cloves, sliced
- 2" (5 cm) ginger root, peeled and finely chopped
- 1 tbsp. tomato paste
- 1 cup (235ml) meat broth
- 1 cinnamon stick
- 2 sweet potatoes, peeled and cut into 1-inch (2.5 cm) cubes

Method:
1. Firstly, take a small bowl and add the salt, pepper, cumin and coriander. Stir well then rub over the lamb. Place to one side as you prepare the other ingredients.
2. Put the olive oil in the bottom of your Instant Pot, turn on the sauté setting and add the meat. Cook until browned on all sides, then pop to one side.
3. Lower the heat and cook the onion until soft, followed by the garlic, ginger and tomato paste. Cook for a further minute.
4. Now add the meat broth and cinnamon and pop the meat back into the pot.
5. Pop the lid on top, seal and cook on high for 25 minutes.
6. Allow the pressure to release naturally, then carefully open the lid and add the sweet potatoes.
7. Put the lid back on, seal once again and cook on high for 10 minutes.
8. Do a quick release then open the lid and serve.
9. Enjoy!

Moroccan Lamb Tagine

Prunes might seem an unlikely choice for this lamb tagine, but they add a sticky sweetness that you just can't get with raisins or apricots (although you can, of course, use them if you wish!) The spice rub is absolutely delicious, and I'd encourage you to try it out with other meats too. Mmm....

Serves: 4

Ingredients:
- 1 tsp. ground cinnamon
- 1 tsp. ginger
- 1 tsp. turmeric
- 1 tsp. cumin
- 2 cloves garlic, crushed
- 3.5 tbsp. olive oil, divided
- 2.5 lbs. (1.2 kg) lamb shoulder, cut into pieces
- 2 medium onions, sliced
- 1 cup (250ml) vegetable stock
- 1 bay leaf
- 1 cinnamon stick
- 1 ½ tsp. salt
- 1 tsp. pepper
- 10 oz. (300g) pitted prunes, soaked
- 3 tbsp. honey
- 3.5 oz. (100g) almonds, shelled, peeled and toasted
- 1 tbsp. sesame seeds

Method:
1. Start by finding a small bowl and mixing together the cinnamon, ginger, turmeric, cumin and garlic. Add 2 tablespoons of the olive oil and stir well to create a paste.
2. Cover the lamb generously with this paste and pop to one side.
3. Next put 1 tbsp. olive oil in the bottom of your Instant Pot, turn on the sauté setting and add the onions. Cook until soft, then remove from the pan.
4. Add a little extra olive oil then add the meat, browning on all sides.
5. Add the stock and stir well to combine, then add the onions, bay leaf and cinnamon.
6. Pop the lid on top, seal and cook on high for 25 minutes.

7. When the time is up, allow the pressure to release naturally then carefully open the lid.
8. Add the salt and pepper, the (drained) prunes, and the honey and give it all a nice stir. Don't forget to take out the bay leaf and the cinnamon.
9. Serve with sprinkled almonds and sesame seeds, and enjoy!

Lamb Rogan Josh

Don't be put off by the long list of spices in this recipe- it's much easier that you think and it's well worth the extra effort for the tender, creamy spiced lamb at the end. If you're worried, simply replace the spices (to which I've added a star) with 3-4 tablespoons of curry powder.

Serves: 4

Ingredients:

For the lamb...

- 1 lb. (450 g) leg of lamb, deboned and cut into cubes
- 4 tbsp. Greek yogurt
- ½ tsp. Garam masala

For the sauce...

- 1 tbsp. olive oil
- 2 bay leaves*
- 3 green cardamom pods, cracked open*
- 1-2 inches (2-5cm) cinnamon bark*
- 2 whole cloves*
- 1.5 tsp. cumin seeds*
- 1.5 tsp. fennel seeds*
- 2 cloves of garlic, minced
- ½ tsp. garam masala**
- ½ tsp. ground chili (to taste)**
- 1 tsp. ground coriander**
- 1 tsp. ground cumin**
- 1 tsp. ground ginger**
- 2 tomatoes, diced
- 2 tbsp. tomato purée
- 100 ml (1/2 cup) water (adjust to taste)
- 1 tbsp. fresh coriander, chopped
- Salt, to taste

Method

1. Let's start by making the marinade. Take a bowl, combine the yogurt and garam masala and stir well. Then stir through the lamb, cover and pop into the fridge for 24 hours.
2. Pour the olive oil into the bottom of your Instant Pot, turn on the sauté setting.
3. Add the first group of spices*. Cook briefly so the flavors really start to release.
4. Add the garlic and stir well, then add the remaining spices**. Cook for another minute or two, then add the tomatoes, tomato puree and water.
5. Remove the lamb from the fridge and add this to the Instant Pot too.
6. Now place the lid on top, seal, cancel the sauté and cook on high for 10 minutes.
7. Do a natural pressure release and then carefully remove the lid.
8. Switch onto sauté again and reduce the sauce down until it thickens.
9. Add sprinkle with fresh coriander, extra seasoning then serve and enjoy.

TIP: This tastes even better popped into the fridge overnight and eaten the next day.

Greek Lamb Beef Gyros

This Greek-style meatloaf is bursting with herbs and garlic, and will take you right back on holiday. When it comes to serving, you can enjoy whatever you like with it- why not try the suggestions on the list?

Serves: 4

Ingredients:
- 2 lbs. (900g) ground lamb or beef
- 1 small onion, chopped
- 8 cloves garlic
- 2 tsp. dried marjoram
- 2 tsp. rosemary
- 2 tsp. oregano
- 2 tsp. salt
- ¼ tsp. ground pepper

To Serve...
- 2 cups (490g) Tzatziki sauce
- Feta Cheese
- Fresh Tomatoes, chopped
- Onions, sliced
- Greek Pitta
- Lettuce
- Cucumber

Method:
1. Start by chopping the onions well then placing into a clean tea towel and squeezing as much of the moisture out as possible.
2. Place into your food processor, along with the garlic, marjoram, rosemary, oregano, and seasonings. Blend well.
3. Now add the meat and hit that whizz button until everything is combined well.
4. Now take a loaf pan and grease well with oil. Place the meat mixture into the pan and press down well. Cover with tin foil.
5. Open up your Instant Pot, insert the trivet and put some water, then place the lid, seal and cook on high pressure for 15 minutes.
6. Do a natural pressure release before carefully opening the lid and removing the loaf pan.
7. Leave to cool for 15 minutes, then carefully remove and slice thinly.
8. Serve and enjoy!

Lamb Stew Provencal

Give your lamb a French touch with this wine, rosemary and pearl barley scented dish. I love how wholesome it is, whilst still keeping that authentic French 'je ne sais quoi'.
Enjoy!

Serves: 4 - 6

Ingredients:
- ¾ cup (90g) flour
- Salt and pepper, to taste
- 1 lb. (450g) lamb, diced
- 2 tbsp. olive oil
- 1 shallot, chopped
- 1 tsp. garlic, minced
- 1 cup (235ml) dry red wine
- 4 cups (940ml) beef broth/stock
- 2 bay leaves
- 1 sprig fresh rosemary
- 1 tbsp. Herbes de Provence
- 1 cup (150g) pearl onions
- 2 cups (150g) mushrooms
- 4 cups (600g) root vegetables
- Flat leaf parsley (garnish)

Method:
1. Grab a large bowl and add the flour, salt and pepper. Stir well to combine, then add the lamb on top. Stir well until the meat is well coated.
2. Now open your Instant Pot, add the olive oil and turn the heat up to medium.
3. Add the lamb, the shallot and the garlic. Cook gently until the meat starts to brown.
4. Next add the red wine, stock, bay leaves, rosemary and herbs and stir well to combine everything.
5. Pop the lid on top, seal and cook on high pressure for 30 minutes. Meanwhile prep the veggies.
6. When the timer sounds, do a quick pressure release, open up, add the veggies and close quickly again. Seal and cook on high for a further 10 minutes.
7. Allow a natural pressure release, then open the lid carefully, serve and enjoy.

Irish Lamb Stew

The Irish do their stews like no other- dark, heavy and satisfying! Enjoy this one, with its obligatory bottle of Guinness (or Stout) and plenty of root veggies to help keep you warm throughout the most difficult of winters.

Serves: 4-6

Ingredients:
- 2 tbsp. olive oil
- 2 lbs. (940g) leg of lamb, trimmed of excess fat and cut into cubes
- Salt and freshly-ground black pepper, to taste
- 2 large onions, chopped
- 2 garlic cloves, minced
- 1 x 12 fl. oz. (350ml) bottle dark stout beer, divided
- 1 tsp. chicken bouillon granules
- 1 tbsp. dried thyme
- 1 bay leaf
- 1 x 32 oz. (950ml) chicken stock
- 5 to 6 large red potatoes, cubed
- 2 to 3 large carrots, peeled and sliced
- 2 large leeks, sliced
- 1 turnip, chopped into chunks
- ¼ cup (5g) fresh parsley, chopped (garnish)

Method:
1. Open up your Instant Pot, add the olive oil and switch onto sauté.
2. Season the meat with salt and pepper then pop into the pot and cook until brown. Remove from the pot and place to one side.
3. Now add the onions and garlic and cook until soft.
4. Add the stout and the bouillon and stir it up well. Allow it to come to a boil then add the lamb back into the pot, followed by the thyme, bay leaves and enough stock to cover the meat.
5. Pop on the lid, seal and cook on high for 30 minutes. Once the timer sounds, allow the pressure to naturally release, then carefully open.
6. Now add the potatoes, carrots, leeks and turnips, stir well then pop that lid back on.
7. Seal, and cook on high for a further 10 minutes, then do a quick pressure release.
8. Open up that lid, add extra seasoning and garnish with extra parsley.
9. Serve and enjoy!

Lamb Shanks

This recipe has a secret ingredient...do you know what it is? No?? Then you'll just have to make it and see. The flavor will surprise you, as will the tenderness of the meat, the richness of the gravy and the love that you can practically taste!

Serves: 4

Ingredients:
- 4 lamb shanks
- 1 large onion, diced
- 2 medium carrots, diced
- 4 cloves garlic, diced coarsely
- 1 tbsp. balsamic vinegar
- 1/2 cup (120ml) red wine
- 1 cup (235ml) beef bone broth or beef stock
- 1 x 15oz (425g) diced tomatoes
- 1 tbsp. fish sauce
- 1 tsp. dried thyme
- 2 bay leaves
- 1 tbsp. sea salt
- 2-3 tbsp. olive oil
- 1-2 tbsp. chopped parsley (optional)

Method:
1. Start by placing the oil into your Instant Pot and turning onto sauté. Add the lamb and cook until brown on all sides, then pop onto a place.
2. Now add the onions, carrots and garlic to your Instant Pot and cook until soft.
3. Add the balsamic vinegar and the wine and stir well. Allow it to reduce slowly before adding the broth, tomatoes, fish sauce, thyme and bay leaves. Give it all a nice stir to combine.
4. Finally add the lamb back into the pot, pop on the lid, seal and cook on high for 45 minutes.
5. Once the timer sounds, allow the pressure to release naturally then carefully remove the lid.
6. Remove the bay leaves and lamb then turn the pot onto sauté mode. Stir and reduce the sauce.
7. Place your lamb onto a place and then pour the gravy lovingly over the top.
8. Enjoy!

BBQ Pulled Pork

This BBQ pork takes slightly longer than the other recipes, but it's definitely worth the effort! Try it and you'll see! It's sticky, slightly smoky, garlicky and altogether WOW!

Serves: 6-8

Ingredients:

- 3-4 pounds (1.3kg-1.8kg) boneless pork, cut into cubes
- 2 tbsp. smoked paprika
- 1 tbsp. brown sugar
- 2 tsp. garlic powder
- 1 tsp. freshly-ground black pepper
- 1 tsp. ground mustard
- 1 tsp. salt
- 1 tbsp. olive oil
- 2 cups (470ml) BBQ sauce, divided
- 1 cup (235ml) chicken stock or water

Method:

1. Start by taking a large bowl and combining the paprika, sugar, garlic, pepper, mustard and salt. Mix well.
2. Then add the pork to the bowl and coat well with the spices. Pop into the fridge overnight to allow the flavors to combine.
3. Now press sauté on your Instant Pot, add a little oil then add the pork. Brown well and pop onto a plate. Turn your pot off.
4. Place the pork back into the pot, followed by the stock and half of the BBQ sauce. Stir well then pop the lid on top and seal.
5. Cook on high for 60 minutes, then allow the pressure to release naturally and carefully open the lid.
6. Remove the pork but leave the sauce, then turn your pot back onto sauté and allow the sauce to simmer for 10 minutes.
7. Shred the pork using forks, then add back into the pot and stir well to combine.
8. Serve and enjoy with the rest of the BBQ sauce.

Chinese Pork Tenderloin

Have you ever taken a bite of a recipe and thought to yourself 'where have you been all my life??' That's exactly what I thought when I pulled this out of my Instant Pot for the first time, and exactly what has me so hooked to the Instant Pot now. Just try it!

Serves: 4-6

Ingredients:
- 2 lbs. (900g) pork tenderloin
- 1 cup (235ml) beef broth, divided in half
- ¼ cup (50g) brown sugar
- 2 tsp. salt
- 1.5 tsp. Chinese Five Spice, divided into 1 tsp and 1/2 tsp
- ½ tsp. paprika
- 2 tbsp. soy sauce
- 1 tbsp. sherry
- ¼ cup (60ml) + 1 tablespoon of hoisin sauce, divided
- 1 tbsp. garlic, minced
- ½ tbsp. ginger, chopped
- 1 tsp. white miso paste (optional)
- 1/3 cup (115g) honey
- 2 tbsp. corn starch + 2 tbsp. water (to form a corn starch slurry)

Method:
1. Start by taking a large mixing bowl and adding all the ingredients except the honey and corn starch. Only use ½ cup broth at this point, 1 teaspoon of the Five Spice and 1 tablespoon hoisin sauce. Stir well to combine.
2. Add the pork to the bowl then stir well. Cover and pop into the fridge for 24 hours to allow the flavors to combine.
3. Now open your Instant Pot and add the contents of the bowl with the remaining broth, hoisin sauce, Five Spice and the honey. Mix well.
4. Pop on the lid, seal and cook on high for 8 minutes.
5. When the timer sounds, allow the pressure to release naturally and carefully remove the pork, placing onto a nice serving dish.
6. Pour the liquid through a strainer and then pop back into the Instant Pot. Turn onto high and allow it to start bubbling. Then add the corn starch and water mix, and stir well to combine.
7. Pour this sauce over the pork and then serve and enjoy!

Garlicky Cuban Pork

This one is another hands-off, leave to cook and enjoy kind of meal. For best results, you'll need to leave to marinade in your fridge overnight, but it's well worth the effort.

Serves: 6-8

Ingredients:
- 3 lbs. (1.3 kg) boneless pork shoulder blade roast, lean, all fat removed
- 6 cloves garlic
- Juice of 1 grapefruit
- Juice of 1 lime
- ½ tbsp. fresh oregano
- ½ tbsp. cumin
- 1 tbsp. kosher salt
- 1 bay leaf

To serve...
- Lime wedges
- Chopped cilantro
- Hot sauce
- Tortillas
- Salsa

Method:
1. Start by placing all the ingredients except the pork and the bay leaf into the food processor and whizzing until smooth.
2. Cut the pork into four pieces, place into a large bowl and pour the sauce on top. Pop into the fridge overnight for the flavors to combine nicely.
3. The next day, transfer to the Instant Pot, add bay leaf on top, and pop on the lid and seal.
4. Cook on high pressure for 60 minutes, then allow the pressure to release naturally.
5. Carefully remove the lid, then remove the pork, shredding carefully.
6. Pour the sauce over the pork then serve and enjoy!

Easy Pork Chops in Mushroom Gravy

This all-in-one pork chop dish is a great option for those evenings when you're too busy to eat but your stomach is growling. Take ten minutes to set it up, leave it for a further ten or so and you're ready to eat. Yum!

Serves: 4

Ingredients:
- 4 bone-in pork chops, thin/medium cut
- 1 tbsp. salt
- 2 tbsp. corn starch
- 2 tbsp. olive oil
- ½ cup (75g) onions, sliced
- 2 cloves garlic, minced
- 2 tbsp. sherry (optional)
- 8 oz. (225g) Cremini Mushrooms
- Baby Bella mushrooms, sliced
- 1 ¼ cups (300ml) chicken broth

For the gravy...
- 1 cup (235ml) milk
- 1 tbsp. corn starch
- 1 ½ tbsp. butter (at room temperature)
- Salt and pepper, to taste

Method:
1. Start by grabbing a big bowl and mixing together the ingredients for the gravy, then pop to one side.
2. Now take your pork and season with salt and roll over corn starch.
3. Turn your Instant Pot onto sauté, add some oil and allow it to warm.
4. Add the pork chops, cooking until brown on all sides. Remove and place to one side.
5. Now place the onions and garlic into the pan and sauté for a few minutes, before adding the sherry. Stir well.
6. Add the gravy mixture to the pan and stir well, then add the mushrooms and the pork.
7. Pop on the lid, seal and cook on high for 8 minutes.
8. Allow the pressure to release naturally then carefully open the lid.
9. Remove the pork, cover with the gravy and enjoy!

Hawaiian Kalua Pork

This pork is really something special. With liquid smoke, soy sauce and sugar, you'll end up with a sticky pulled pork that puts the rest to shame!

Serves: 4

Ingredients:
- 1 tbsp. olive oil
- 2 lbs. (900g) pork roast
- ½ cup (120ml) water
- 2 tbsp. Wright's Hickory Liquid Smoke
- 2 tbsp. soy sauce
- 2 tbsp. brown sugar
- ½ tbsp. salt

Method:
1. Start by putting your Instant Pot onto sauté, adding the olive oil and then placing the pork into the pan. Brown on all sides, then place on one side.
2. Add the water, liquid smoke, soy sauce and brown sugar and stir well to combine, followed by the pork and salt.
3. Pop on the lid, seal and cook on high for 60 minutes.
4. When the timer sounds, allow the pressure to release naturally, then carefully open the lid.
5. Remove the meat from the pan, shred and serve.
6. Enjoy!

Pork Tenderloin Teriyaki

What can I say? Pork + Teriyaki = HEAVEN!! This recipe only serves two, but can be easily doubled if you have a larger crowd to feed.

Serves: 2

Ingredients:
- 2 pork tenderloins
- Salt and pepper, to taste
- 2 tablespoons oil
- 2 cups (470ml) teriyaki sauce
- Toasted sesame seeds, to taste
- 2 green onions, sliced

Method:
1. Start by seasoning your pork with salt and pepper, then place to one side.
2. Put some oil into your Instant Pot, turn on to sauté then add the pork when hot. Brown on all sides, then pour the teriyaki sauce over the top.
3. Pop on the lid, seal and cook on high for 20 minutes.
4. Allow the pressure to release naturally then carefully remove the lid.
5. Remove the meat from the pot, slice and serve with toasted sesame seeds and the chopped onions.
6. Enjoy!

Sweet Balsamic Glazed Pork Loin

You can even do a pork loin roast in your Instant Pot! Yes, I know- this book really does keep getting better! Sweet and sticky with a hint of sage, this will melt in your mouth and leave you wondering why it took you so long to invest in an Instant Pot.

Serves: 4-6

Ingredients:
For the pork...
- 2 - 3 lbs. (900-1.3kg) boneless pork loin or pork sirloin roast, trimmed
- 1 tsp. dried sage
- 1 clove garlic, minced
- ½ tsp. coarse salt
- ½ tsp. coarse black pepper
- 1 cup (240ml) water or chicken broth

For the glaze...
- ½ cup (100g) brown sugar
- 1 tbsp. corn starch
- ¼ cup (60ml) balsamic vinegar
- ½ cup (120ml) water
- 2 tbsp. soy sauce
- Salt and pepper, to taste

Method:
1. Start by combining the sage, garlic, salt and pepper in a bowl and mixing well. Then add the pork, rubbing the seasoning in well.
2. Now place the pork into the Instant Pot, add the water or broth and pop on the lid.
3. Seal then cook on high for 60 minutes.
4. When the timer sounds, allow the pressure to release naturally and remove the pork. Shred the meat into pieces and place onto a platter.
5. Meanwhile, place the glaze ingredients into a saucepan and placing over a heat. Whisk well and allow it to thicken. Add a touch of salt and pepper then pour over the meat.
6. Serve and enjoy!

Jamaican Jerk Pork Roast

This one is sooo simple. You don't even need to leave it to marinade, simply spice your meat and start cooking. Your family is going to love you forever when they taste this.

Serves: 12

Ingredients:
- 4 lbs. (1.8kg) pork shoulder
- 1 tbsp. olive oil
- 4 tbsp. Jamaican Jerk spice blend
- ½ cup (120ml) beef stock or broth

Method:
1. Start by brushing the meat with olive oil, then covering with the Jamaican spice blend.
2. Turn on your Instant Pot to sauté then add the meat. Brown on all sides.
3. Add the beef broth, cover with the lid, seal, then cook on high for 45 minutes.
4. Allow the pressure to release naturally, then serve and enjoy!

Jamaican Goat Curry

Goat is very common meat in Jamaica and much of Africa, but if often doesn't get served often around here. And I really think that's a shame because not only does goat curry contain so much tropical love, it's the kind of soul food that we should all be eating more of.

Serves: 4-6

Ingredients:
- 1 tbsp. cumin seeds*
- 1 tbsp. coriander seeds*
- 1 tbsp. all spice berries*
- 2 tsp. yellow mustard seeds*
- 1 tsp. fenugreek seeds*
- 2 tsp. white peppercorns*
- 2-3 cloves garlic, minced*
- 2 tsp. ground ginger*
- 3 tbsp. curry powder
- 2 tsp. Thai chili powder or cayenne
- 3 tsp. turmeric powder
- 3 tbsp. oil
- 2 lbs. (900g) goat chops
- 3 cups (450g) onions, diced
- 4-5 cloves garlic
- 3-4 sprigs of thyme
- 2 green onions, chopped
- Salt, to taste
- 2 cups (470ml) water
- 2 russet potatoes

Method:
1. Place the whole spices* into a pan and toast, then grind and place into a bowl. Add the remaining spices then set to one side.
2. Turn your Instant Pot onto sauté and add oil and the goat chops, browning on all sides. Once done, remove from the pot and set to one side.
3. Now place the onions into the pan and cook until soft.

4. Add the goat back to the Instant Pot with the spice mixture, garlic, thyme, green onions, salt and water, then stir well.
5. Pop the lid on top, seal then cook on high for 25 minutes.
6. Meanwhile, peel the potatoes, dice and place into a bowl. Cover with oil and thyme, then place into a 400°F (200°C) oven until done.
7. When the timer sounds, allow the pressure to release naturally, open carefully and add those potatoes. Cook until the potatoes are soft.
8. Serve and enjoy!

Poultry

Chicken & Rice Burrito Bowls

This must surely be the easiest dinner on the planet. Just throw it all in, give it a stir and leave it to cook! And not just that- it also takes pretty amazing if you ask me.

Serves: 4- 6

Ingredients:
- 1 ½ tbsp. vegetable oil
- 1 medium onion, diced
- 2 cloves garlic, minced
- 1 tbsp. chili powder
- 1 ½ tsp. ground cumin
- 1 cup (235ml) chicken broth, divided
- 1 ½ lbs. (675g) boneless, skinless chicken thighs
- Salt and pepper, to taste
- 1 cup (185g) long-grain white rice
- 1 x 15 oz. (425g) can black beans, drained and rinsed
- 1 cup (175g) frozen corn kernels
- 1 x 15 oz. (425g) jar salsa
- ½ cup (60g) cheddar cheese, shredded
- ¼ cup (15g) fresh cilantro, chopped

Method:
1. Start by pouring the oil into your Instant Pot and turn onto sauté. Add the onion and garlic and cook until soft.
2. Next stir in the chili powder and cumin and cook for a few seconds more.
3. Now add ¼ cup of the chicken broth and stir well to combine. Leave to simmer for a few minutes.
4. Meanwhile, prepare your chicken. Sprinkle with salt and pepper, then place into the Instant Pot, along with the rice, beans, corn, salsa and the rest of the broth.
5. Cover with the lid, seal and cook on high for 10 minutes.
6. When the timer sounds, do a quick pressure release then carefully remove the lid.
7. Stir well then ladle into bowls, top with cheese and cilantro and enjoy!

Honey Sesame Chicken

Honey and sesame seeds are two ingredients that deserve to be crowned the ultimate food ever- I'm addicted to those little crunchy snack bars. So, this chicken recipe is really my dream come true! Thanks to the addition of the sticky Chinese-style sauce, it's amazing!

Serves: 6

Ingredients:
- 4 large boneless skinless chicken breasts, diced
- Salt and pepper, to taste
- 1 tbsp. vegetable oil
- ½ cup (75g) diced onion
- 2 cloves garlic, minced
- ½ cup (120ml) soy sauce
- ¼ cup (60ml) ketchup
- ¼ tsp. red pepper flakes
- 2 tsp. sesame oil
- 2 green onions, chopped
- 1/2 cup (170g) honey
- 2 tbsp. corn starch
- 3 tbsp. water
- Sesame seeds, toasted

Method:
1. Start by seasoning the chicken with salt and pepper then place to one side.
2. Meanwhile, pour the oil into your Instant Pot and turn onto sauté. Add the onion and garlic and cook until soft. Then add the chicken and stir well.
3. Now add the soy sauce, ketchup and red pepper flakes and stir well to combine.
4. Cover with the lid, seal and cook on high for 3 minutes.
5. When the timer beeps, do a quick pressure release and carefully remove the lid.
6. Stir through the sesame oil, green onions and honey.
7. Combine the corn starch and water in a small bowl and carefully stir through.
8. Turn back onto simmer and cook until the sauce thickens, and sprinkle the sesame seeds.
9. Serve and enjoy!

Southwestern Chicken and Rice

This chicken and rice dish is very simple, but don't be deceived- it's mouth-wateringly good. It also keeps really well so you can enjoy any leftovers for your lunch the following day. Feel free to add whatever extra toppings you fancy- extra chili is always my vote!

Serves: 4

Ingredients:
- 1 ½ cups (285g) brown rice
- ¾ cup (200g) salsa
- 1 x 15 oz. (425g) can kidney beans, drained and rinsed
- ½ cup (60g) frozen corn
- 1 ½ cups (350ml) chicken stock
- 2 chicken breasts
- 1 tsp. chili powder
- ½ tsp. garlic powder
- ½ tsp. onion powder
- ¼ tsp. cumin
- ½ tsp. salt
- ½ cup (60g) cheddar, shredded

To serve...
- Chips
- Hot sauce
- Shredded cheese

Method:
1. Open your Instant Pot and add the brown rice, salsa, kidney beans, corn and chicken stock then stir well to combine.
2. Add the chicken breasts and press down below the water level.
3. Top with chili powder, garlic and onion powder, cumin and salt then stir through.
4. Now pop on the lid and cook on high for 25 minutes.
5. Allow the pressure to release naturally for 10 minutes then do a quick pressure release.
6. Carefully open the lid and remove the chicken. Cut into small pieces. Fluff the rice then add the chicken back and shredded cheese, and mix well.
7. Top with cheese, hot sauce and chips.
8. Serve and enjoy!

Chicken Cacciatore

This chicken is so versatile- I love it over rice, pasta, polenta, baked potatoes, or even with a side serving of toast. Mmmm tomatoes, peppers and onions...mmmm...

Serves: 4-6

Ingredients:
- 4 chicken thighs, with the bone, skin removed
- Salt and fresh pepper, to taste
- 1 tbsp. olive oil
- ½ cup (75g) onion, diced
- ¼ cup (45g) red bell pepper, diced
- ½ cup (90g) green bell pepper, diced
- ½ x 14 oz. can (210g approx.) crushed tomatoes
- ½ tsp. dried oregano
- 1 bay leaf
- 2 tbsp. chopped basil

Method:
1. Start by seasoning the chicken with salt and pepper, then pop to one side.
2. Turn the Instant Pot onto sauté, add the oil and pop the chicken inside, cooking until browned on all sides. Pop to one side.
3. Then add more oil into the pot and add the onions and pepper, then cook for 5 minutes until soft.
4. Add the chicken, tomatoes, oregano, bay leaf, salt and pepper, then stir well.
5. Pop the lid on top, seal and cook on high for 25 minutes.
6. When the timer beeps, allow the pressure to release naturally then carefully open the lid.
7. Remove the bay leaf and sprinkle with basil, then serve and enjoy!

Mom's Chicken Curry

This isn't just any old curry- this is a real-life Indian mother's chicken curry as shared with me by one of my closest friends. Whilst the list of spices is long, it's easy to make and tastes great. That chicken will really be melting in your mouth. Enjoy!

Serves: 4

Ingredients:
- 1 lb. (450g) chicken, boneless, cut into chunks
- 3 tbsp. oil
- 1 black cardamom*
- 6 black peppercorns*
- ½ tsp. cumin seeds*
- 1 green chili, chopped (optional)
- 1 medium onion, chopped
- 1" (2.5cm) ginger, chopped
- 5 cloves garlic, chopped
- 2 medium tomatoes, chopped
- 2 bay leaves
- 6 garlic cloves
- 2 tsp. coriander
- ½ tsp. cayenne
- ½ tsp. Garam masala
- ¼ tsp. turmeric
- 1 tsp. salt
- ½ cup (120ml) water
- 1 tbsp. lemon juice

To serve...
- Cilantro

Method:
1. Start by pouring some oil into the Instant Pot and turn onto sauté.
2. Add the whole spices* and cook for 30 seconds to allow them to release their flavor.
3. Next add the chili, onions, ginger and garlic and cook for a further 4 minutes until soft.
4. Next add the tomatoes and the remaining spices, stirring through and cooking for a minute or two.

5. Then add the chicken pieces and cook for another couple of minutes, then add the water.
6. Pop on the lid, seal and cook on high for five minutes.
7. When the timer beeps, do a quick pressure release and open the lid carefully.
8. Stir through the lemon juice then serve and enjoy!

Honey Garlic Chicken

Garlic? Honey? Chicken? OMG – yes please!

Serves: 2-4

Ingredients:
- 1 ½ lbs. (675g) chicken breast, cut into cubes
- 1 tbsp. olive oil
- 2 tbsp. water
- 3 tsp. corn starch

For the sauce...
- 2 green scallions, thinly sliced
- 6 tbsp. honey
- 3 garlic cloves, minced
- 1 tsp. onion powder
- ½ tsp. garlic powder
- 1 ½ tbsp. soy sauce
- ½ tbsp. Sriracha sauce

Method:
1. Start by placing all the sauce ingredients into a bowl and stirring well until combined.
2. Then open up your Instant Pot, adding the olive oil and turn onto sauté. Add the chicken and cook for 1-2 minutes to seal the edges.
3. Now pour the sauce over the chicken, pop the lid on top, seal and cook on high for 3 minutes.
4. When the timer beeps, do a quick pressure release and open carefully.
5. Now make slurry by mixing the corn starch and water in a bowl then stir well to dissolve. Add this to the Instant Pot and stir through.
6. Turn your Instant Pot back to sauté and heat until the sauce thickens.
7. Serve and enjoy!

Chili-Lime Chicken

The classic combo of chili and lime in this Latin-inspired dish mean that it will work really well for all kinds of South American dish, tastes out of this world when sliced and enjoyed in a sandwich and will get your tongue dancing with flavor. Adjust the chili powder according to taste.

Serves: 4

Ingredients:

- 2 lbs. (900g) boneless, skinless chicken breasts
- 2 medium limes
- 1 tsp. salt
- ¼ tsp. black pepper
- ½ tsp. liquid smoke
- 6 cloves garlic, minced
- 1 ½ tsp. chili powder
- 1 tsp. cumin
- 1 tsp. onion powder

Method:

1. Start by giving your chicken some TLC by cutting in half if they're thick pieces. Then place into your Instant Pot.
2. Pour the juice from both limes over the top, sprinkle over the seasonings, liquid smoke and garlic then rub the spices into the chicken.
3. Pop on the lid, seal and cook on high for 6 minutes.
4. When timer beeps, allow a natural pressure release for 5 minutes then do a quick release.
5. Shred the chicken, put back into the pot, pour the juice in the pot over the chicken, season with salt and pepper.
6. Serve and enjoy!

Roasted Moroccan Chicken

Everyone loves tucking into a freshly roasted chicken which has been lovingly coated with a carefully-balanced mix of spices, then roasted to crunchy perfection. So, you'll definitely want to make this one next time you fancy something inspiring! Yum!

Serves: 4-6

Ingredients:
- 4 tbsp. olive oil
- ½ tsp. cumin
- 1 ½ tsp. coriander
- 1 ½ tsp. paprika
- 1 ½ tsp. yellow curry powder
- ½ tsp. crushed red pepper flakes
- 3 cloves garlic, minced
- 1 tsp. ginger powder
- Fresh parsley, leaves only
- 4 tsp. lemon juice
- Salt and pepper, to taste
- 1 whole chicken
- 1 ½ cups broth

Method:
1. Take a medium bowl and add all the ingredients, except for the chicken and broth. Stir well to combine, then add salt and pepper to taste.
2. Rub this mixture over the chicken and pop into the fridge overnight to allow the flavors to blend.
3. Now open your Instant Pot and add a drop of olive oil, then turn onto sauté.
4. Pop the chicken into the pot and sear on the outside.
5. Then add the broth, pop the lid on the top, seal and cook on high for 25 minutes.
6. When the timer beeps, allow a natural pressure release for 25 minutes. Then do a quick pressure release and carefully remove the lid.
7. Remove the chicken, serve and enjoy!

Mongolian Chicken

Do your nomadic thing with this very special Mongolian chicken dish. It's ready very fast and contains a balance of flavors which is like a super-healthy version of Chinese food. Serve it with rice, noodles or whatever else you desire.

Serves: 6

Ingredients:
- 2 tbsp. extra virgin olive oil
- 4 boneless skinless chicken breasts, cut into cubes
- 2 tbsp. corn starch
- 1 cup (200g) brown sugar
- 8-10 garlic cloves, minced
- 1 tbsp. fresh ginger minced
- 1 cup (235ml) soy sauce
- 1 cup (235ml) water
- 1 cup (150g) carrots, chopped
- 1 tsp. red pepper flakes
- 1 tbsp. garlic powder
- ¼ cup (60g) green onions, chopped (optional)
- 1 tsp. sesame seeds

Method:
1. Start by turning your Instant Pot onto sauté and adding the oil.
2. Place the chicken into a large bowl and add the corn starch, stirring well to combine. Now pop the chicken into the Instant Pot and cook for 2-3 minutes, stirring often.
3. Next add the rest of the ingredients, and stir well.
4. Cover with the lid, seal and cook on high for 10 minutes.
5. When the timer sounds, allow the pressure to release naturally for 10 minutes then do a quick release.
6. Carefully open up and turn on the sauce function. Stir well until the sauce thickens, then serve and enjoy!

Turkey Breast with Gravy

Turkey is one of those meats that often gets forgotten, unless it's served up at Thanksgiving, then eaten as leftovers for the next few weeks. But when you try this delicious meal, you'll wonder why you haven't been eating more of the stuff. Thanks to the delicate balance of thyme and garlic, plus a thick and delicious sauce, you'll love this any night of the week.

Serves: 6-8

Ingredients:

- 6.5 lb. (3kg) bone-in, skin-on turkey breast
- 1 tsp. garlic powder
- 1 tsp. onion powder
- ½ tsp. paprika
- Salt and pepper, to taste
- 1 large onion, quartered
- 1 stock celery, cut in large pieces
- 3 cloves of garlic
- 1 sprig of thyme
- 1 tbsp. olive oil
- 1 x 14 oz. (415ml) turkey or chicken broth
- 3 tbsp. corn starch
- 3 tbsp. cold water

Method:

1. Start by taking a large bowl and adding the garlic powder, onion powder, paprika, salt and pepper. Stir well to combine then add the turkey and rub spices over the turkey.
2. Now take another bowl and add the onion, celery, garlic and thyme then mix well to combine. Stuff the turkey with this mixture.
3. Pour the olive oil into the Instant Pot and turn onto sauté, then add the turkey and brown on all sides.
4. Add the chicken broth then cover with the lid, seal and cook on high for 30 minutes.
5. When the timer sounds, allow the pressure to naturally release for 10 minutes, then do a quick pressure release.
6. Open the lid carefully and remove the turkey.

7. Take a small bowl and mix together the corn starch and water, then slowly add to the Instant Pot.
8. Switch onto sauté and warm gently until thickens.
9. Serve the chicken with the sauce, and enjoy!

Turkey and Sweet Potato Chili

Whip up a super-fast, super-filling chili with this turkey and sweet potato recipe. The addition of garbanzo beans is a genius extra which really balances texture and taste, and gives you something nutritious to sink your teeth into. Adjust the chili according to taste, and feel free to add extra chili sauce if it's still not hot enough when it makes it to the table.

Serves: 6

Ingredients:
- Olive oil
- 1 medium brown onion, diced
- 3 cloves garlic, minced
- 1 lb. (450g) turkey, minced
- 1 x 14.5 oz. (450g) diced tomatoes
- 1 x 14.5 oz. (450g) tomato sauce
- 1 x 14.5 oz. (450g) garbanzo beans, drained
- 1 medium red bell pepper, chopped
- 1 medium sweet potato, peeled and chopped
- 1 cup (235ml) vegetable stock
- 1 tsp. cumin
- 1 tsp. paprika
- ½ tsp. chili powder
- Salt and pepper, to taste

Method:
1. First add the oil to the Instant Pot and turn onto sauté. Add the onions and cook until soft.
2. Next add the garlic and sauté and cook for a minute or two, followed by the turkey mince. Cook until brown.
3. Then add the tomatoes, tomato sauce, garbanzo beans, bell pepper, sweet potatoes, veg stock, cumin, paprika, chili, salt and pepper. Mix well.
4. Pop the lid on top, seal and cook on high for 9 minutes.
5. Once the timer sounds, do a quick pressure release and open the lid carefully.
6. Serve and enjoy!

Four-Ingredient Barbecue Turkey

For the fastest, simplest turkey dinner, you can't go wrong with this recipe. You can make it with the ingredients you already having in your pantry and get a nutritious meal on the table before the kids start eating each other!

Serves: 2

Ingredients:
- 2 turkey breasts
- 8 cups (1.8 liters) water
- ¼ cup (75g) salt
- Salt and pepper, to taste
- 1 cup (235ml) apple cider
- 1 tsp. chicken bullion
- Barbecue Sauce

Method:
1. Start by mixing the water with salt and placing the turkey breast inside. Pop into the fridge for at least 4 hours, preferably overnight.
2. Now take the turkey from the fridge, dry well and remove the skin. Season with salt and pepper.
3. Pour the apple cider vinegar and bouillon into the Instant Pot, place the steaming rack inside and pop the turkey on the rack.
4. Pop the lid on top, seal, and cook on the meat setting for 45 minutes.
5. When the timer beeps, do a quick release and take the turkey from the Instant Pot, placing onto a plate.
6. Brush the turkey with the barbecue sauce and pop under your grill until it goes sticky.
7. Serve and enjoy!

Teriyaki Turkey Meatballs

Mmmm...you got to love those meatballs! I love this version because they're Asian-inspired, melt-in-the-mouth and they're pretty good for you too. Enjoy!

Serves: 4

Ingredients:
For the meatballs...
- 1 lb. (450g) ground turkey meat
- 1 tsp. garlic powder
- 5 saltine crackers
- 3 tbsp. buttermilk
- ¼ cup (40g) green onion
- ½ tsp. kosher salt
- Black pepper to taste
- 1 tbsp. canola oil
- 1 tbsp. sesame seeds

For the Teriyaki Sauce...
- ½ cup (120ml) soy sauce
- ¼ cup (60ml) rice vinegar
- 2 cloves garlic, minced
- 2 tsp. fresh grated ginger
- 2 tbsp. canola oil
- 3 tbsp. brown sugar
- ¼ tsp. black pepper
- 1 tbsp. corn starch

Method:
1. Start by taking a large bowl and adding the turkey, garlic powder, crackers, buttermilk, green onions, salt and pepper. Mix well and form into meatballs. The mixture will make 16 meatballs.
2. Now take the teriyaki sauce ingredients and put them into a medium bowl. Mix and set aside.
3. Add the oil to the Instant Pot, turn onto sauté and pop the meatballs into the bottom. Brown on all sides.
4. Add the teriyaki sauce then pop the lid on top of the Instant Pot, seal and cook on high for 10 minutes.
5. When the timer beeps, do a quick pressure release then carefully open the Instant Pot.
6. Serve and enjoy with sprinkled sesame seeds!

Turkey Spinach Lasagna

Turkey probably isn't the meat you'd consider when it comes to making lasagna, but it works incredibly well. The rich meat balances well with the acidity of the tomatoes and the creamy ricotta and mozzarella cheese so you have a delicious meal to remember.

Serves: 6

Ingredients:
- 1 tbsp. olive oil
- 1 lb. (450g) ground turkey
- 1 tsp. dried Italian seasonings
- ½ tsp. salt and red-pepper flakes to taste
- 15 oz. (425g) ricotta
- 1 ½ cups (185g) mozzarella, shredded
- 10 oz. (280g) frozen chopped spinach, thawed and drained
- Salt and freshly ground pepper
- 1 large jar chunky pasta sauce
- 6-9 oven-ready lasagna noodles, broken to fit
- 1 cup (235ml) water

Method:
1. Pour olive oil into the Instant Pot, switch onto sauté and add the turkey.
2. Stir well until brown, then add the Italian seasonings, salt and pepper flakes.
3. Put the ricotta, 1 cup mozzarella and spinach into a bowl, season with salt and pepper, then stir well to combine.
4. Find an oven-proof dish that will fit inside the Instant Pot and add a spoonful of pasta sauce to coat the bottom, followed by a layer of noodles.
5. Add about half of the meat mixture, followed by the pasta sauce, followed by half the cheese mixture.
6. Repeat the layers, then sprinkle the top with ½ cup mozzarella. Cover the dish with foil.
7. Now pour the water into the Instant Pot and place the trivet into the bottom.
8. Place your oven-proof dish onto the Instant Pot, cover with the lid, seal and cook on high for 20 minutes.
9. When timer beeps, do a quick pressure release then carefully remove the lid.
10. Remove the foil, then let it sit for a few minutes before serving and enjoying!

Rosemary Duck Ragu

This duck Ragu isn't the fastest of the recipes to make, but your Instant Pot makes a long job much faster. It tastes perfect with bread and salad, rice, veggies or whatever else you feel like eating. Delicious!

Serves: 2

Ingredients:
- 2 duck legs, skin on bone in
- 2 star anise
- 2 cloves garlic, crushed
- 2 stems fresh rosemary
- 1 rib celery
- 1 small red onion
- 2 tablespoons tomato purée
- 3 tablespoons Marsala wine
- Sea salt and black pepper, to taste

Method:
1. We need to give the duck some TLC (Tender, Loving Care) first. Pop the duck legs onto a plate and slash the skin several times.
2. Next open the Instant Pot, turn onto sauté setting and add the duck legs. Cook for 10 minutes, turning often to brown the fat.
3. Cancel the sauté mode, pour off the fat (save it for later) then return the duck to the pot with the star anise, garlic cloves, and a stem of rosemary. Pour over enough water to just cover the duck.
4. Cover with the lid, seal and cook on high for 45 minutes.
5. Meanwhile, pop the celery and onion into the food processor and pulse until fine, adding the rest of the rosemary at the last step.
6. When the timer beeps, do a quick pressure release, then carefully open the lid.
7. Remove the duck legs and pour off the water and herbs, but retain the garlic.
8. Turn the pot back onto sauté and add some of the duck fat, followed by the chopped onion and celery mixture, and cook for 2-3 minutes. Add the tomato puree followed by the Marsala wine.
9. Meanwhile, shred the duck then add to the pot.
10. Season well then serve and enjoy!

BBQ Duck

This slow-cooked duck recipe is absolutely incredible. The slow cooking allows the duck to become soft and tender, the BBQ rub adds that rich warming flavor and the veggies turn a meat into an entire meal. Make it the night before and enjoy!

Serves: 4-6

Ingredients:
- 1 whole duck, quartered
- 1 tsp. sea salt
- 1 tsp. ground black pepper
- 2 tbsp. BBQ rub
- 4-5 large carrots, roughly chopped
- 1 lb. (450g) butternut squash, cubed
- 1 onion, sliced into rings
- 1 head garlic, cut in half lengthwise and peeled
- ½ cup (120ml) water
- 1 tbsp. apple cider vinegar

Method:
1. Start by placing the duck onto a plate, slashing the skin with a knife and rub with salt, pepper and BBQ rub, then set to one side.
2. Now open your Instant Pot and place the root veg, onion and garlic into the bottom, followed by the water.
3. Rest the duck on top of the veggies then add the water and cider vinegar and cover with the lid.
4. Seal and cook on low for 10-12 hours, until soft.
5. Do a quick pressure release then carefully open the lid.
6. Remove the duck and transfer to a lined baking sheet then roast in a preheated oven on 400° F (205° C) until crispy and yum.
7. Serve and enjoy!

Fish

Chinese-Style Steamed Ginger Scallion Fish

Fish is wonderful to cook in the Instant Pot because it's so fast! Blink and it's done! For best results, you'll want to marinade the fish in the fridge overnight, but then all you need to do is take it out and start cooking- your meal will be ready in less than ten minutes.

Serves: 4

Ingredients:
- 1 lb. (450g) firm white fish such as Tilapia
- 3 tbsp. soy sauce*
- 2 tbsp. rice wine*
- 1 tbsp. Chinese black bean paste*
- 1 tsp. minced ginger*
- 1 tsp. garlic*
- 2 tbsp. julienned ginger, sliced thinly
- ¼ cup (60g) green onions/scallions, chopped
- ¼ cup (10g) cilantro, chopped
- 2 cups (470ml) water
- 1 tbsp. peanut oil

Method:
1. Start by placing the fish onto a plate. Combine the sauce ingredients* in a bowl then pour over the fish. Leave for 30 minutes to marinade.
2. Meanwhile, chop the veggies and pop them to one side.
3. Next open up your Instant Pot, add the water, insert the steamer then pop the fish into the steamer basket. Don't throw away that marinade- pop it to one side.
4. Cover with the lid, seal and cook on low for 2 minutes. Do a quick pressure release.
5. Grab a saucepan, add the oil then fry the ginger, scallions, and cilantro then cook for a couple of minutes. Add the marinade you reserved and stir well to combine.
6. Allow it to boil until cooked, then pour over the fish.
7. Serve and enjoy!

Coconut Fish Curry

This Asian coconut fish curry is lightly creamy, spicy, and oh-so moreish. Like the other fish recipes here, it's ready fast and in your tummy before you can say 'take me to Thailand!'

Serves: 4

Ingredients:
- 1-1.5 lbs. (500-750g) fish steaks or fillets, cut into bite-size pieces
- 1 tbsp. olive oil
- 6 bay leaves
- 3 tbsp. curry powder
- 2 medium onions, sliced into strips
- 2 garlic cloves, squeezed
- 1/8 tsp. ginger powder
- 2 cups (470ml) coconut milk
- 2 green chilies, sliced into strips
- 1 tomato, chopped
- Salt, to taste
- Juice of ½ lemon

Method:
1. Start by adding the olive oil to your Instant Pot, turning the heat to sauté and dropping in the bay leaves. Fry until golden, then add the onion, garlic and ginger and sauté until soft.
2. Next add the curry powder and stir through. Cook for a further two minutes.
3. Pour in the coconut milk, the green chilies, tomatoes and fish pieces. Stir well to coat.
4. Cover with the lid, seal, and cook on high for five minutes.
5. Do a natural pressure release, carefully open the lid, add salt and extra lemon juice, then stir well.
6. Serve and enjoy!

Fish and Potato Chowder

The secret of any brilliant fish chowder is the freshness of the fish- don't skimp when it comes to buying good quality, wild-farmed fish if you care about great tasting food, and also your health. Combined with the black pepper, bacon and butter, you'll have a meal to remember.

Serves: 4

Ingredients:

- 2 cups (470ml) water
- 1 2/3 lbs. (750g) white fish
- 1 cup (225g) Yukon Gold Potato, peeled and diced
- ½ cups (75g) celery, diced
- ¾ cups (105g) onion, diced
- 1/8 tsp. salt
- 1/8 tsp. black pepper
- 1/8 tsp. garlic powder
- 2/3 cups (150ml) chicken broth
- 2 tbsp. bacon, cooked and diced
- 1 1/3 cups (315ml) milk
- 1/3 cups (70g) Instant Potatoes
- 2/3 tbsp. butter

Method:

1. Start by placing the water into your Instant Pot with the fish, potatoes, celery, onions, salt, pepper, garlic powder, chicken broth, bacon and milk. Stir well to combine.
2. Place the lid on top, seal and cook on high for 10 minutes.
3. Allow the pressure to naturally release, then do a quick release to let the rest go.
4. Open up the lid carefully, then add the butter and the potato flakes (Instant Potatoes).
5. Turn onto sauté then cook gently for 5 minutes until thick and yummy!
6. Serve and enjoy!

Wild Alaskan Cod

Simple, delicious and ready quickly. What more could you want?

Serves: 4

Ingredients:
- 2 cups (300g) cherry tomatoes
- 2 large cod fillets, cut into 2-3 pieces
- Salt and pepper, to taste
- 4 tbsp. butter
- Olive oil
- 1 cup water

Method:
1. Find an oven-safe baking dish that fits into your Instant Pot.
2. Add the tomatoes, followed by the fish, and the seasoning.
3. Pop the butter on top and drizzle with olive oil.
4. Place the trivet into the Instant Pot, add a cup of water to the bottom and place the oven-proof dish inside.
5. Close the lid, seal and cook on high for 5-7 minutes.
6. When the timer beeps, do a quick pressure release then carefully open the lid.
7. Serve and enjoy!

Mediterranean Rosemary Salmon

Served steaming from your Instant Pot, you'll feel like you're still on your European holiday, soaking up the sun, eating fresh cherry tomatoes from the vine and drinking copious amounts of red wine... Mmmm...

Serves: 2-3

Ingredients:
- 1 cup water
- 1 lb. (450g) wild salmon, frozen
- 1 sprig fresh rosemary
- 10 oz. (280g) package fresh asparagus
- ½ cup (75g) cherry tomatoes, cut in half
- 2 tbsp. olive oil
- 1 lemon, juiced (optional)
- Salt and pepper, to taste

Method:
1. Start by placing the wire rack into the bottom of your Instant Pot and pour the water inside.
2. Now add the frozen salmon, the rosemary and the fresh asparagus.
3. Cover with the lid, seal and cook on high for 3 minutes.
4. Do a quick pressure release once the timer beeps, then carefully open the lid.
5. Remove the fish, pop onto a place and add the tomatoes, drizzle extra olive oil over the top, squeeze a little lemon over the top.
6. Season then serve and enjoy!

Vietnamese Halibut Hot Pot (Ca Kho To)

You really can't go wrong with Asian fish dishes, and this one is certainly no exception. It's fast, it's spicy, sweet and most of all, tastes AMAZING!

Serves: 2-4

Ingredients:
- 1.6 lbs. (750g) halibut
- 1 cup (150g) caster sugar
- 3 tbsp. Asian fish sauce
- 3 cloves of garlic, chopped
- 2" (5cm) fresh ginger, chopped
- 5 shallots, chopped
- 1 bunch spring onions, chopped
- 2 whole red Thai chilies
- Freshly ground black pepper
- 2/5 cup (100 ml) water
- 1 splash groundnut oil
- 1 2/3 cups (400 ml) coconut water

Method:
1. Start by chopping the fish and placing it into a medium bowl.
2. Add 1/3 cup (50g) of the sugar, fish sauce, garlic, ginger, shallots, spring onions, chilies and some ground black pepper. Add to the fish and marinate.
3. Meanwhile, let's make some caramel sauce by placing 2/3 cup (100g) sugar into a saucepan, pour over the water and bring to the boil. Continue to boil for 10 minutes.
4. Now open your Instant Pot, turn onto sauté and add the oil. Then add the fish and cook for 2-3 minutes on each side.
5. Pour over the marinade, caramel sauce, and coconut water, then close the lid and seal.
6. Cook on high for 5 minutes, then do a quick pressure release. Open the lid carefully.
7. Add a touch more coconut water if needed and serve and enjoy!

Seafood Gumbo

Combining fresh flavors and plenty of Southern taste, this gumbo sticks to the tradition of keeping it simple whilst giving your taste buds exactly what they want (even if they don't realize it at the time!)

Serves: 4-6

Ingredients:
- 24 oz. (680g) sea bass, cut into chunks
- Salt and pepper, to taste
- 3 tbsp. Cajun seasoning
- 3 tbsp. olive oil
- 2 yellow onions, diced
- 2 bell peppers, diced
- 4 celery sticks, diced
- 28 oz. (680g) diced tomatoes
- 4 tbsp. tomato paste
- 3 bay leaves
- 1 ½ cups (350ml) bone stock
- 2 lbs. (900g) medium to large raw shrimp, deveined

Method:
1. Pop the sea bass into a bowl and season well with salt, pepper and half of the Cajun seasoning. Stir well until everything is coated.
2. Now place the oil into your Instant Pot, press sauté and add the fish. Cook on all sides for around 4 minutes. Remove from the pan and place onto a plate.
3. Add the onions, pepper, celery, and the rest of the seasoning then cook for a minute or two to allow the flavors to release.
4. Then add the diced tomatoes, tomato paste, bay leaves and bone broth. Stir well.
5. Cover with the lid, seal then cook on high for 5 minutes.
6. Once the timer beeps, do a quick pressure release.
7. Switch onto sauté, add the shrimps and cook for 3-4 minutes until the shrimps change color.
8. Season with extra salt and pepper, then serve and enjoy!

Fifteen-Minute Asian Salmon & Vegetables

For those of you who like to pile up the veggies and enjoy omega-3 rich fish, you'll want to try this one tonight. It's very easy, fast and you can switch up the veggies you include so it takes even better. Just try it!

Serves: 2

Ingredients:

For the fish...
- 1 cup water
- 2 medium fillets of salmon or other fish
- 1 clove of garlic, finely diced
- 2 tsp. of grated ginger
- ¼ long red chili, finely diced
- Sea salt and pepper
- 2 tbsp. soy sauce or gluten-free tamari sauce
- 1 tsp. honey

For the vegetables...
- 8 oz. (225g) mixed green vegetables (string beans, broccoli, snow peas)
- 1 large carrot, sliced
- 1 clove of garlic, diced
- Juice ½ lime
- 1 tbsp. tamari sauce
- 1 tbsp. olive oil
- ½ tsp. sesame oil (optional)

Method:
1. Open the Instant Pot and place the steamer rack inside. Now add the water.
2. Next find an oven-proof bowl that fits inside the Instant Pot and set to one side.
3. Take each fillet of fish and cover with the garlic, ginger and chili, plus some extra salt and pepper, and put into the bowl.
4. Find a small bowl, add the soy sauce and honey, mix well, then pour over the fish.
5. Place the bowl inside the Instant Pot, cover and seal.
6. Cook on high for 3 minutes.
7. Meanwhile prepare the veggies by chopping and sprinkling with chopped garlic, then placing them into a steamer basket.
8. Once the timer beeps, do a quick pressure release and carefully open the lid.

9. Place the steamer basket on top of the bowl containing the fish, drizzle with lime juice, tamari sauce, olive oil and sesame oil, plus a small amount of salt and pepper.

10. Cover with the lid, seal and cook on high for 0 minutes (it will take some time for steam to get to high temperature, and by the time it does, the fish will be nicely steamed and cooked) .

11. When the timer beeps, wait for 1 minute, do a quick pressure release then carefully remove the lid.

12. Take everything out, serve and enjoy!

Four- Minute Salmon, Broccoli & Potatoes

Yes, you just need four minutes to create this fast, tasty dinner! It's simple, delicately flavored with butter and fresh herbs and will be ready and on the table in the blink of an eye.

Serves: 2

Ingredients:
- 3.5 lbs. new potatoes
- Salt & pepper, to taste
- Fresh herbs (optional)
- 2 salmon fillets
- 2 cups (140g) broccoli, chopped
- 160ml water
- 2 tsp. butter

Method:
1. Start by popping your potatoes into a large bowl and cover with salt, pepper and fresh herbs (optional, but really add to that flavor!). Stir well to combine.
2. Next sprinkle your salmon and broccoli with your salt and pepper.
3. Now pour the water into the bottom of your Instant Pot and add the steaming rack.
4. Add the potatoes, topped with a knob of butter and replace the lid.
5. Seal and cook on the steam setting for 2 minutes, then do a quick release and open the lid.
6. Now add the broccoli and salmon, cover again, seal and cook for 2 more minutes.
7. When it beeps, allow a natural pressure release then serve and enjoy!

Seafood

Quick Seafood Paella

Seafood paella in less than 30 minutes? You got it. This one even lets you create your own fish stock for added flavor, although you can replace this with a premade cube if you prefer. You'll need to let it stand for an hour if you want best results, but it's equally good when served immediately. You decide.

Serves: 4

Ingredients:
For the fish stock...
- 4 white cod heads
- 2 carrots
- 1 stick of celery
- 1 bay leaf
- 6 cups (1.4 liters) water
- Fresh parsley, chopped

For the paella...
- 4 tbsp. olive oil
- 1 yellow onion, diced
- 1 red bell pepper, diced
- 1 green bell pepper, diced
- Large pinch saffron threads
- 2 cups (370g) white rice
- 1 cup (180g) seafood such as squid, meaty white fish, scallops
- 1/8 tsp. ground turmeric
- 2 tsp. sea salt
- 2 cups (350g) mixed shellfish such as clams, mussels, shrimp

Method:
1. Start by making the fish stock. This is really easy – just add the stock ingredients to your Instant Pot, cover, seal and cook on high for 5 minutes.
2. When the timer beeps, allow the pressure to release naturally, then pour into a jug and keep to one side.
3. Now add the olive oil to your Instant Pot, turn onto sauté then add the onions and peppers, and cook until soft.

4. Add the saffron, rice and seafood and sauté together for a couple of minutes.
5. Then add the stock you made earlier, turmeric and salt and mix well. Pop the shellfish on top.
6. Now close the Instant Pot, seal and cook on high for 6 minutes.
7. When the timer beeps, allow the pressure to release naturally, then open the lid.
8. Give the paella a stir, put back the lid on and leave to stand for 1 hour.
9. Serve and enjoy.

Cajun Shrimp and Sausage Boil

If you're looking for pure Louisiana flavor, you can't go wrong with this smoked sausage, corn, shrimp and crab stew. Fast, furious and very tasty, it will fuel you for anything!

Serves: 4

Ingredients:
- ½ lb. (225g) smoked sausage, cut into four pieces
- 4 ears fresh corn
- 2 red potatoes, cut in half
- 1 tbsp. Louisiana Shrimp and Crab mix
- Boiling water, to cover the above
- ½ lb. (225g) raw shrimp

For sauce...
- 6 tbsp. butter
- 1 tbsp. garlic, minced
- 1/8 tsp. Cajun seasoning
- ¼ tsp. Old Bay seasoning
- 3-5 shakes hot sauce
- 1/8 tsp. lemon pepper
- Juice of 1/2 lemon

Method:
1. Start by placing the sausage, corn and potatoes into your Instant Pot and cover with water.
2. Next add the Louisiana Shrimp and Crab mix, cover with the lid, seal and cook on high for 4 minutes.
3. Whilst this is cooking, add the butter to a pan and pop onto your stove over a medium heat.
4. Add the garlic and stir well, then add the rest of the spices.
5. When the timer beeps, do a quick pressure release and carefully open the lid.
6. Add the shrimp to the pot, and stir, then watch them closely. Once they turn pink remove them, along with the corn, potatoes and sausage.
7. Slowly add these into the sauce you made, stirring well to coat.
8. Serve and enjoy!

Restaurant-Style Seafood Chowder

You're probably looking at the list of spices here and thinking 'WOW!' but don't let that put you off. They turn an average seafood chowder into something that will blow your mind. If you don't have all of the spices already, then why not ask your neighbor? Then invite them to join you.

Serves: 4

Ingredients:

- 1 lb. (450g) shrimp or scallops
- 4 tbsp. butter
- 1 cup (150g) onion chopped
- 3 cloves fresh garlic, minced
- 4 cups (950ml) chicken stock
- 2 cups (250g) corn kernels
- 2 cups (300g) carrots, chopped
- 8 oz. (225g) Cremini mushrooms, cut in half
- 2 cups (300g) string beans, cut in half
- 1 lb. (450g) potatoes, peeled and cubed
- 4 tbsp. Dry Sherry
- 1 fresh lemon, sliced
- ½ cup (120ml) heavy whipping cream

Seasonings/Spices...

- 2 ½ tsp. ground celery seed
- 2 ½ tsp. ground mustard seed
- ¼ + 1/8 tsp. allspice
- 1/8 +1/16 tsp. cardamom powder
- 1/8 +1/16 tsp. ground cinnamon
- ¾ tsp. paprika
- Pinch ground ginger
- Salt and pepper, to taste
- Fresh parsley, opt
- 2 bay leaves

Method:

1. Start by opening your Instant Pot, adding the butter and turning onto sauté.
2. Add the onions and garlic and cook for three minutes.
3. Turn off the heat, add ½ cup of the broth, followed by the veggies, the sherry, the lemon and all of the seasonings. Stir well then add the rest of the broth.
4. Cover with the lid, seal and cook on high for 7 minutes.
5. When the timer beeps, allow the pressure to release naturally, then open up.
6. Add the shrimp or scallops, stir well and turn the Instant Pot onto sauté.
7. Add the cream, stir through then serve and enjoy!

Japanese Seafood Curry

This Japanese-style curry contains curry roux, which is an ingredient you'll find in most Japanese homes- pop to your local Asian supermarket and you should find it there. If not, simply substitute with regular curry powder. It will still be tasty!

Serves: 4

Ingredients:
- 12 manila clams
- 2 x 3" (5 cm approx.) kombu
- 3 cups (720ml) water
- 1 tbsp. olive oil
- 3 onions, chopped
- 2 cloves garlic
- 1" (2.5cm) fresh ginger
- 6 oz. (170g) medium size shrimp
- 6 oz. (170g) bay scallop
- 6 oz. (170g) calamari
- ¼ cup (60ml) white wine (opt)
- 6 mushrooms, sliced
- 1 package Japanese curry roux
- Freshly ground black pepper
- 1 tbsp. soy sauce
- ¼ apple, grated

Method:
1. Start by washing the clams carefully by scrubbing them under cold water.
2. Now place the wire rack inside a large bowl and place the clams inside (without overlapping).
3. Next mix 2 cups water with 1 tablespoon salt and mix well. Pour this over the clams then cover with foil and leave in a cool place for 3 hours.
4. Throw away the water, fill with fresh water and leave again for a further hour.
5. Meanwhile we can make the stock by combining the kombu with the 3 cups of water.
6. Next open up your Instant Pot, press the sauté button and add the oil.
7. Add the onion, garlic and ginger and cook for a minute or two.

8. Then add the seafood and the wine, then the stock you just made. Finally, add the mushrooms.
9. Next add the curry roux and black pepper, stir well, then pop on the lid and seal.
10. Cook on high for 5 minutes.
11. Do a quick pressure release then carefully remove the lid.
12. Add the soy sauce and apple, then stir well, serve and enjoy!

Vegetarian & Vegan

Turkish Split Pea Stew

This is one of the most filling stews I've ever tasted, and it's probably one of the most unexpectedly delicious too. You'll warm your tummy and keep your soul happy too. Simply serve with a big chunk of bread, and you have an entire meal in itself.

Serves: 4

Ingredients:
- 1 ½ tbsp. olive oil
- 1 medium white onion, diced
- 1 medium carrot, diced
- 1 celery stick, diced
- 4-5 cloves garlic, diced finely
- 1 bay leaf
- 1 tsp. paprika powder
- 1 ½ tsp. cumin powder
- ½ tsp. salt
- ¼ tsp. cinnamon powder
- ¼ tsp. chili powder
- 2 cups (450g) split yellow peas
- ½ cup (100g) chopped tinned tomatoes
- Juice of ½ lemon
- 7 cups (1 ¾ liters) vegetable stock

Method:
1. Open up the Instant Pot, turn onto sauté setting and add the oil.
2. Throw in the onion, carrot and celery and cook on high for 4 minutes.
3. Add the rest of the ingredients then cover with the lid, seal and cook on high for 10 minutes.
4. When the timer sounds, allow the pressure to release naturally for 5 minutes then do a quick pressure release.
5. Carefully open the lid, serve and enjoy!

Coconut Quinoa Curry

This vegan coconut curry is amazing because you can just throw all the ingredients in and return shortly afterwards when it's cooked, fragrant and ready to eat. Packed with super-foods like quinoa, sweet potato and broccoli, this is healthy, plant-friendly and yum!

Serves: 6-8

Ingredients

- 1/2 cup water
- 1 medium sweet potato, peeled and chopped
- 1 large broccoli head, cut into florets
- ½ white onion
- 1 x 15 oz. (425g) can chickpeas, drained and rinsed
- 1 x 28 oz. (790g) can diced tomatoes
- 2 x (14.5 oz. (410g) can coconut milk
- ¼ cup (47g) quinoa
- 2 garlic cloves, minced
- 1 tsp. ground ginger
- 1 tsp. ground turmeric
- 2 tsp. tamari sauce
- 1 tsp. miso (optional)
- 1/2 – 1 tsp. chili flakes

Method:

1. Simply open the Instant Pot, add the water then throw in the rest of the ingredients.
2. Stir everything well until combined, cover with the lid, seal and cook on high for 5 minutes.
3. When the timer sounds, do a quick pressure release then open the lid carefully.
4. Serve and enjoy!

Red Lentil, Sweet Potato and Hemp Burgers

When it comes to making plant-based burgers, most of the work comes from cooking the veggies in the first place. Thankfully, your Instant Pot can take the hard work out of it, so you can enjoy succulent, healthy veggies burger faster.

Makes: 8-10 patties

Ingredients:
- Olive oil
- 1 cup (150g) minced onion
- 1 teaspoon dried ginger
- 1 cup (75g) minced mushrooms
- 1 cup (200g) red lentils, rinsed and picked over
- 1 medium sweet potato, peeled and cut into large pieces
- 2 ¼ cups (590m) vegetable stock
- ¼ cup (40g) hemp seeds
- ¼ cup (5g) fresh flat leaf parsley, finely chopped
- ¼ cup (5g) fresh cilantro, finely chopped
- 1 tbsp. curry powder
- 1 cup (90g) oats
- 1-4 tbsp. flour, if needed

Method:
1. Open up your Instant Pot, turn onto sauté and add the oil.
2. Throw in the onion, ginger and mushrooms and cook for 4 minutes until the onions gets soft.
3. Add the lentils, sweet potatoes and stock and stir well to combine.
4. Pop the lid on top, seal and cook on high for 6 minutes.
5. When the timer sounds, allow the pressure to release naturally, then open the lid carefully.
6. Leave for 15 minutes, until cool.
7. Now preheat your oven to 375°F/ 190°C and cover a baking sheet with greased parchment paper.
8. Once the veggies are cool, mash them well then stir in the hemp seeds, parsley, cilantro, curry powder and oats. Stir everything well to combine.
9. Form into 8-10 patties (add flour if the mixture is too wet) and place onto the baking sheet and bake for 10 minutes.
10. Allow it to cool then serve and enjoy!

Vegan Lentil Bolognaise

Beluga black lentils are something very special, and I'd highly recommend that you try them if you haven't already. Feel free to replace with regular green lentils if you want to create a fast vegan meal that tastes amazing. Serve with regular pasta or zoodles.

Serves: 2-4

Ingredients:
- 1 cup (200g) Beluga black lentils, washed
- 1 x 28 oz. (790g) can fire roasted chopped tomatoes
- 1 yellow onion, diced
- 4 cloves garlic, minced
- 3 medium carrots, diced
- 1 small can tomato paste
- 4 cups (940ml) water
- 2 tbsp. Italian seasonings
- Red pepper flakes, to taste
- Salt and pepper, to taste

Method:
1. Open up your Instant Pot and all of the ingredients. Stir well to combine then close the lid and seal.
2. Cook on high for 15 minutes.
3. Allow the pressure to release naturally when the timer beeps, then carefully open the lid.
4. Serve and enjoy!

Spinach Garbanzo Bean Chana Masala

Garbanzo beans teamed with spinach make the best ever veggie curry your heart could desire. Even non-vegetarians will swoon! Enjoy!

Serves: 6-8

Ingredients:
- 3 tbsp. cooking oil
- 1 cup (150g) chopped onions
- 1 bay leaf
- 1 green chili, finely chopped
- 1 tbsp. grated garlic
- ½ tbsp. grated ginger
- 1 tbsp. Chana masala
- ½ tsp. turmeric
- 2 tsp. chili powder
- 1 tsp. coriander powder
- 1 tbsp. flour
- 2 cups (450g) tomato puree
- 1 cup (200g) raw garbanzo beans, soaked
- 1.5 cups (350ml) water
- 2 cups (60g) baby spinach, chopped
- Salt, to taste

Method:
1. Start by opening your Instant Pot, turn onto sauté and add the oil.
2. Throw in the onions and cook for 4 minutes until soft.
3. Now add the bay leaf, green chili, ginger and garlic and stir well. Cook for 30 seconds.
4. Throw in the Chana masala, turmeric, chili, coriander and 1 tablespoon water and stir well.
5. Add the flour, then the tomato puree, the garbanzo beans and the water, and stir well again.
6. Cover with the lid, seal and cook on high for 15 minutes.
7. When the timer sounds, allow the pressure to release naturally, then after 15 minutes do a quick pressure release.
8. Carefully open the lid and give it a stir.
9. Then pop back onto sauté, add the spinach and salt, then stir well.
10. Serve and enjoy!

White Bean Stew with Winter Squash and Kale

You can replace the white beans with pretty much any beans in this winter stew. It's perfect for cold fall lunchtimes or evenings, it's a great dish to use up leftover pumpkin from Halloween and, well, brilliant any time of year.

Serves: 6

Ingredients:
- Olive oil
- 1 large onion, diced
- 4 cloves garlic, minced
- 1 lb. (450g) dried yellow-eye or navy beans
- 5 cups (1.1 liters) water
- 4 tsp. smoked paprika
- 2 tsp. dried oregano
- 1 ½ tsp. ground cumin
- 1 tsp. dried basil
- 1 lb. (450g) winter squash or pumpkin, chopped into chunks
- 1 large red bell pepper, diced
- 1 jalapeño pepper, sliced
- 1 x 15oz (425g) can diced tomatoes
- 1 tsp. salt
- 1 bunch kale
- 1 cup (125g) fresh or frozen corn
- ½ cup (60g) fresh basil, chopped

Method:
1. Start by opening the Instant Pot, turn onto sauté and add the oil.
2. Add the onions and cook for around 4 minutes until soft, then add the garlic.
3. Throw in the beans, water, paprika, oregano, cumin and basil, then cover with the lid, seal and cook on high for 8 minutes.
4. Once the timer beeps, do a quick release then open.
5. Now add the squash, peppers, jalapeño, tomatoes and salt then stir well.
6. Cover with the lid, seal and cook on high for 8 minutes.
7. Allow the pressure to release naturally then open the lid carefully.
8. Add the kale, corn and basil, turn back onto sauté and heat until the kale softens.
9. Serve and enjoy!

Lentil Kidney Bean Chili

Pop kidney beans and lentils together, throw in some chili spice and tomato, add a few extras and liven up your life. The touch of Mexican combined with vegan goodness is certainly a winner!

Serves: 2

Ingredients:
- 1 tablespoon olive oil
- ½ red onion, chopped
- 1 green chili, chopped
- Freshly ground pepper
- 2-3 cloves garlic, chopped
- 2 medium tomatoes, chopped
- ½ teaspoon chipotle pepper powder
- 2-3 teaspoons taco spice blend
- ½ red bell pepper, chopped
- ¼ cup (40g) chopped celery
- 1 cup (200g) dry lentils, soaked in hot water for 30 minutes
- 1 cup (180g) kidney beans, cooked or canned
- 2 cups (470ml) water (adjust to taste)
- Salt, to taste
- ½ cup (60g) fresh or frozen corn
- Lemon juice

To serve...
- Pickled jalapeno
- Fresh cilantro,
- Sour cream/yogurt
- Guacamole
- Tortilla strips

Method:
1. Take your Instant Pot, turn onto sauté and add the oil. Then throw in the onions and cook for 4 minutes, until soft.
2. Add the green chili, pepper and garlic and cook for 2 minutes more.
3. Then add the tomatoes, chipotle pepper, taco spice and cook for around 5 minutes.
4. Next add the bell pepper and celery then mix and cook for another minute.

5. Finally drain the lentils and throw then into the pot, followed by the kidney beans, salt and water, then mix well.
6. Add the lid, seal and cook on high for 5 minutes.
7. Do a quick pressure release then open the lid.
8. Turn back onto simmer and add the corn and lemon juice.
9. When the sauce thickens, serve and enjoy!

Creamy Vegan Veggie Pasta

You don't have to quit those creamy pasta dishes when you're vegan- just create this vegan veggie pasta instead. For a cheesy note, you can even add some nutritional yeast, but honestly- I think it's awesome without.

Serves: 4

Ingredients:
- 3 cups (700ml) vegetable stock
- 1 x 15 oz. (425ml) can coconut milk
- 1 ½ tsp. salt
- ½ tsp. black pepper
- 1 tsp. parsley
- 1 tsp. onion, chopped
- ½ tsp. garlic powder
- ½ tsp. oregano
- ½ tsp. basil
- ¼ tsp. red pepper flakes (optional)
- 8 oz. (225g) pasta shells
- 2 cups (300g) frozen mixed vegetables like peas, corn, green beans
- 2 cups (60g) spinach

Method:
1. Easy! Place all the ingredients into your Instant Pot, then stir well.
2. Cover with the lid, seal and cook on high for 4 minutes.
3. When the timer beeps, do a quick pressure release then carefully open the lid.
4. Serve and enjoy!

Vegan Quinoa Burrito Bowls

Yay for fast quinoa burrito bowls. They're very simple, taste great and make a wonderful lunch or dinner. You can replace the quinoa with regular rice if you prefer, and add as many extras as you like.

Serves: 4

Ingredients:
- 1 tsp. extra-virgin olive oil
- ½ red onion, diced
- 1 bell pepper, diced
- 1 tsp. ground cumin
- ½ tsp. salt
- 1 cup (190g) quinoa, rinsed
- 1 cup (260g) salsa
- 1 cup (235ml) water
- 1 x 15 oz. (425g) can black beans, drained and rinsed

Method:
1. Open your Instant Pot, add the oil and turn onto sauté.
2. Cook the onions and peppers for 5 to 8 minutes until soft.
3. Then stir through cumin and salt and cook for another minute.
4. Then throw in the quinoa, salsa, water and beans, then cover with the lid, seal and cook on low for 12 minutes.
5. When the timer beeps, let the pressure release naturally.
6. Carefully remove the lid, fluff the quinoa then serve and enjoy!

Vegan Lentil Barbacoa

Another easy one-pot meal, this vegan lentil barbacoa is packed with plant-based nutrition, it's fast and it will keep your tummy happy! Enjoy!

Serves: 2

Ingredients:
- 2 tbsp. olive oil
- ½ white or yellow onion, minced
- 3 cloves garlic, minced
- 1 ½ cups (300 g) cooked green or brown lentils, rinsed
- 1 ½ cups (200g) grated carrots, shredded
- 2-3 tbsp. brown sugar
- Salt and pepper, to taste
- 1 ½ tsp. ground smoked paprika
- 2 tsp. ground cumin
- ¼ tsp. ground cloves
- 1 ½ tsp. dried oregano
- 2-3 chipotle peppers in adobo sauce
- 2 tbsp. soy sauce
- ¼ cup (60 ml) lime juice
- 2 tbsp. (30 ml) vinegar
- ¼ cup (60 ml) water (more as needed)
- 2 bay leaves (optional)

Method:
1. Open the Instant Pot, add the oil then turn on sauté setting.
2. Add the onions and garlic and cook for 4 minutes until soft.
3. Add the remaining ingredients, stir well and cover with the lid.
4. Seal and cook on high for 5 minutes.
5. Do a quick pressure release, carefully open the lid and stir.

Desserts

Stuffed Peaches

Enjoy fresh peaches by filling them with a crumble mixture, which is flavored with almond and cinnamon. The only problem is, can you really wait until they cool enough, or will you just tuck in...?

Serves: 4-6

Ingredients:
- 5 medium peaches
- ¼ cup (30g) flour
- ¼ cup (50g) sugar
- 2 tbsp. butter
- ½ tsp. ground cinnamon
- ¼ tsp. pure almond extract
- Pinch sea salt
- 1 cup (235ml) water
- ¼ tsp. pure almond extract

Method:
1. Slice the tops off the peaches then carefully remove the stones (seeds) from the peaches so they are hollow. Be carefully and make sure you leave the flesh inside. Place to one side.
2. Take a large bowl and add the flour, sugar, butter, cinnamon, almond extract and salt, then mix well to combine.
3. Press this mixture into the peaches and put them aside.
4. Open the Instant Pot and place the steamer basket inside, then add the water and the almond extract.
5. Carefully place the peaches into the steamer basket, then place the lid, seal and cook on high for 3 minutes.
6. When the timer beeps, do a quick pressure release then carefully open.
7. Remove the peaches then leave them to rest for 10 minutes until cool slightly.
8. Serve and enjoy!

Extra-Easy Rice Pudding

Everyone loves rice puddings, but they don't love waiting hours for them to cook to perfection and thicken enough to taste good. But guess what? In an Instant Pot, rice pudding is easy. This one is extra indulgent but you're worth it.

Serves: 3-4

Ingredients:
- 1 cup (185g) basmati rice
- 1 ¼ cups (300ml) water
- 2 cups (470ml) milk
- ¼ cup (320g) maple syrup
- 1/8 tsp. sea salt
- ¾ cup (180ml) heavy cream
- 1 tsp. vanilla extract

Method:
1. Place the rice into your Instant Pot, followed by the water, milk, maple syrup and sea salt. Stir well to combine.
2. Then pop the lid on top, seal and cook on porridge setting. (This should take around 20 minutes.) If you don't have a porridge setting, cook on high for 20 minutes.
3. When the timer beeps, allow the pressure to release naturally for 10 minutes then do a quick pressure release.
4. Open the lid, add the cream and vanilla then stir well.
5. Serve and enjoy!

Wine Poached Figs with Yogurt Cream

Ready for an extra-special dessert to serve when you really want some indulgence? Try these wine-poached figs, topped with yoghurt cream, and sprinkled with pine nuts. Yum!

Serves: 2-4

Ingredients:

For the poached figs...
- ½ cup (70g) pine nuts
- 1 cup (235ml) red wine
- 1 lb. (500g) figs
- ½ cup (100g) sugar

For the yogurt crème...
- 2 lbs. (1 kg) plain yogurt
- Fine mesh strainer

Method:

1. Start by making the yogurt cream. Just place the yogurt into the strainer and spread out well (put a bowl underneath it), then place into your fridge to drain for 4 hours.
2. Meanwhile, toast the pine nuts in the bottom of your Instant Pot.
3. Remove them and place them onto a plate.
4. Now add the wine to the Instant Pot and place the figs inside, standing up.
5. Now cover with the lid, seal and cook on low for 3 minutes.
6. Do a quick pressure release, remove the figs (but leave the wine inside), then make the wine syrup.
7. Pour the sugar into the Instant Pot, stir well and warm on sauté setting until it thickens slightly. Now you're ready to serve.
8. Put as much yogurt as you like onto the plate, followed by the fig, then drizzle the wine syrup over the top. Sprinkle with pine nuts then serve and enjoy!

Molten Chocolate Mini Lava Cake

OMG! This molten chocolate cake is AMAZING. It's so good that you can just whip up a batch whenever the urge to eat one takes hold and enjoy!

Serves: 3

Ingredients:
- 1 cup (235ml) water
- Butter or oil, for greasing
- 1 free-range egg
- 2 tbsp. olive oil
- 4 tbsp. sugar
- 4 tbsp. milk
- 4 tbsp. flour
- 1 tbsp. cocoa powder
- Pinch salt
- ½ tsp. baking powder
- ½ tsp. orange zest, grated

Method:
1. Start by opening your Instant Pot and adding the water. Place the trivet into the bottom.
2. Now find three ramekins, grease with the butter or oil and set aside.
3. Grab a medium bowl, mix the remaining ingredients and stir well.
4. Pour the mixture into the ramekins then place inside the Instant Pot.
5. Place the lid on top, seal and cook on high for 6 minutes.
6. Once the timer beeps, do a quick pressure release and carefully open the lid.
7. Remove the ramekins, sprinkle with powdered sugar (optional) and enjoy!

Salted Caramel Cheesecake

This one takes slightly longer than the deserts so far in this book, but it's definitely worth it when your mouth fills with salted caramel delight. If you're feeling really indulgent, you can add extra chocolate sauce and really make it extra awesome. Yummy!

Serves: 6-8

Ingredients:

For the crust...
- 1 ½ cups (75g) Ritz crackers, crushed
- 4 tbsp. butter, melted
- 2 tbsp. sugar

For the cheesecake...
- 16 oz. (450g) cream cheese, room temperature
- ½ cup (100g) brown sugar
- ¼ cup (30ml) sour cream
- 1 tbsp. flour
- 1/2 tsp. kosher salt
- 1 ½ tsp. vanilla
- 2 free-range eggs

For the topping...
- ½ cup (115g) caramel sauce
- 1 tsp. flaked sea salt

For the Instant Pot...
- 2 cups (470ml) water

Method:

1. Take a 7" (17cm) springform pan and spray lightly with cooking oil. Make sure it fits into your Instant Pot. Cut some parchment paper to fit the bottom and spray. Pop to one side.
2. Grab a large bowl, add the Ritz crumbs, butter and sugar, stir well and press into the bottom of your pre-prepared pan. Set aside.
3. Now take your stand mixer and add the cream cheese and sugar. Beat until everything is combined and even.
4. Add the sour cream and mix again for 30 seconds.
5. Next add the flour, salt and vanilla and stir well.
6. Finally add the eggs, and mix until just smooth.

7. Pour the mixture into your pre-prepared pan.
8. Open the Instant Pot, place the trivet inside the bottom and add the water. Then wrap the pan with foil and use this to lower the spring form pan into the Instant Pot.
9. Close the lid, seal and cook on high for 35 minutes.
10. When the timer beeps, allow the pressure to release naturally then carefully remove the lid.
11. Remove from the Instant Pot and pop into the fridge overnight.
12. Just before serving, pour over the caramel sauce and sprinkle with salt, then serve and enjoy!

Chocolate Cake

This simple chocolate cake makes a fabulous quick birthday treat, it's wonderful to take for afternoon tea with friends and it's great to enjoy when you want a treat. You can also experiment with the recipe and add whatever you want, such as candied orange, mint leaves and so on.

Serves: 6

Ingredients:
- 3 free-range eggs (white and yolk separated), room temperature
- ¾ cup (90g) all-purpose flour
- ¾ cup (90g) cocoa powder
- ½ tsp. baking powder
- 1 ½ cups (190g) powdered sugar
- 2/5 cup unsalted butter
- 1 tsp. vanilla extract

Method:
1. Firstly, separate the egg whites and yolks.
2. Then beat the egg whites until fluffy, followed by the egg yolks.
3. Take a large bowl and add the flour, cocoa powder and baking powder. Stir well to mix.
4. Now take another bowl, add the powdered sugar and butter, then beat until creamy.
5. Next add the egg white to the mixture in 4. and stir well to combine.
6. Now add the egg yolk to 5. and stir well to combine.
7. Next add the vanilla extract and stir through, followed by the flour mixture. Go gently- you don't want to make it lumpy!
8. Line a spring form pan with parchment paper, grease and pour the cake batter inside.
9. Place inside the Instant Pot, cover with the lid, seal and cook on low for 30 minutes.
10. When the timer beeps, do a quick pressure release and carefully open the lid.
11. Serve and enjoy!

Lavender Crème Brûlée

Shhh... this one is very special, just for you. The recipe makes enough for one, but you can, of course double it or even quadruple it to serve a crowd. Love it!

Serves: 1

Ingredients:
- 1/3 cup (80ml) heavy cream
- 1 tsp. sugar
- 1 egg yolk
- 1 tsp. vanilla extract
- Lavender buds, to taste
- 1 cup (235ml) water

To decorate...
- Pinch of food grade organic lavender buds
- 1 tsp. sugar

Method:
1. Take a pan and add the cream and sugar. Stir well to combine then place over a medium heat – stirring until the sugar melts. Cool to room temp.
2. Whisk the egg yolk into the cream mixture, followed by the vanilla extra and a few lavender buds.
3. Pour this mixture into a ramekin.
4. Open the Instant Pot, add the water and place the trivet inside.
5. Now lower the ramekin into the Instant Pot and cook on high for 9 minutes.
6. When the timer buzzes, do a quick pressure release and open the lid carefully.
7. Leave to cool for 45 minutes and then pop into the fridge overnight.
8. When ready to serve, sprinkle with the sugar and broil until brown.
9. Serve and enjoy!

Lemon Poppy Seed Bundt Cake

You'll need to start preparing this lemon poppy seed cake the night before, but let me assure you it's very much worth it for the light, citrus taste. Whip it up, patiently allow it to cook and then tuck in!

Serves: 6-8

Ingredients:
For the lemon poppy seed Bundt cake...
- 2 cups (240g) all-purpose flour
- ¾ tbsp. lemon juice
- 1 ¼ cups (295ml) milk (adjust to taste)
- 4 tbsp. poppy seeds
- ½ cup (100g) coconut oil, barely melted
- 1 ¼ cup (250g) brown sugar
- Pinch sea salt
- 2 free-range eggs
- 2 tsp. baking powder
- 3 tsp. lemon peel, grated

For the lemon syrup...
- 1/3 cup (75ml) lemon juice
- 1/3 cup (65g) brown sugar

For the Instant Pot...
- 2 cups water

Method:
1. Start by grabbing a large bowl and add the flour, lemon juice, milk and poppy seeds then mix well until combined.
2. Cover and leave to sit at room temp for 6-8 hours.
3. Next add the remaining ingredients and stir until combined.
4. Now open up your Instant Pot and place the trivet inside. Add the water and then turn onto sauté.
5. Grease and line a Bundt cake tin, then pour the cake mixture inside, and lower into your Instant Pot.
6. Cover with the lid, seal and cook on high for 50 minutes.
7. When the timer beeps, allow the pressure to release naturally for 10 minutes, then do a quick pressure release.

8. Carefully open the lid, remove the cake and remove the water from the pot, then remove the trivet.
9. Then make the lemon syrup by adding the lemon juice and the sugar into your in Instant Pot, stir well and warm on sauté function. Stir for 2-3 minutes until bubbles then switch off.
10. Poke holes all over the cake then drizzle the syrup over the cake.
11. Serve and enjoy!

Lemon Pudding Cups

Lemon pudding. In a cup. What else can I say but, MAKE THEM!

Makes: 7 cups

Ingredients:
- 3 cups (705ml) milk
- ¼ cup (60ml) lemon juice, room temperature
- 1 ½ tbsp. lemon zest, grated
- ½ cup (160g) maple syrup
- 3 tbsp. coconut oil, room temperature
- 3 free-range eggs, room temperature
- 2 tbsp. gelatin

For the Instant Pot...
- 1 cup water

Method:
1. Grab your blender and add the milk, lemon juice, zest, maple syrup, coconut oil and eggs then blend for a minute. Taste and add more lemon or maple syrup if needed, then blend again.
2. Then remove that little mini lid whilst the motor is still running and slowly add the gelatin. Keep blending until smooth.
3. Pour the pudding into seven glass jars, which hold approximately ½ pint (235ml). Put on the lids.
4. Now open the Instant Pot, add the trivet and add the water.
5. Lower the jars inside, cover with the lid then seal.
6. Cook on high for 5 minutes.
7. When the timer sounds, do a quick pressure release then open the lid carefully.
8. Carefully remove the jars (be careful- they are hot!), and place to one side to cool.
9. Transfer the jars to the fridge to cool.
10. Shake if required then serve and enjoy!

Oreo Cheesecake

I first tried Oreo cheesecake in a hotel and was instantly blown away by it. Of course, from that moment, I wanted to recreate it and tried, and tried and tried but failed. That was, until I found this recipe. It's utterly amazing!

Serves: 6

Ingredients:
For the crust...
- 12 whole Oreo cookies, crushed into crumbs
- 2 tablespoons salted butter, melted

For the cheesecake...
- 16 oz. (450g) cream cheese, room temperature
- ½ cup (100g) granulated sugar
- 2 free-range eggs, room temperature
- 1 tbsp. all-purpose flour
- ¼ cup (60ml) heavy cream
- 2 tsp. pure vanilla extract
- 8 whole Oreo cookies, coarsely chopped

For the topping...
- 1 cup (240ml) cream, whipped
- 8 whole Oreo cookies, coarsely chopped
- Chocolate sauce (opt)

For the pot...
- 1 ½ cup water

Method:
1. Start by preparing your springform pan. Aim for a 7" (17cm), but make sure that it fits your Instant Pot. Spray with cooking spray.
2. Now grab a large bowl and stir the crushed Oreo cookies and melted butter together. Press the crumbs into the bottom of your pan. Pop into the freezer for 10-15 minutes.
3. Place the cream cheese into a large bowl and beat until smooth. Add the sugar and mix again.
4. Add the eggs one by one until it's perfectly mixed.

5. Finally add the flour, cream and vanilla and mix until smooth, then fold in the chopped Oreo cookies and pour everything into the springform pan. Cover with some foil.
6. Open your Instant Pot, place the trivet in the bottom then add the water.
7. Create a foil sling and lower your springform pan into the bottom of the Instant Pot.
8. Cover with the lid, seal and cook on high for 40 minutes.
9. When the timer beeps, allow the pressure to release naturally for 10 minutes then do a quick pressure release.
10. Carefully open the lid then remove the cheesecake from the Instant Pot.
11. Cool to room temp then pop into the fridge overnight.
12. Serve and enjoy!

Keto Almond Carrot Cake

If you're following a Keto diet or you're eating gluten-free, you're going to LOVE this almond-carrot cake recipe. It's moist, spicy and so indulgent.

Serves: 8

Ingredients:
- 3 free-range eggs
- 1 cup (100g) almond flour
- 2/3 cup (135g) sugar
- 1 tsp. baking powder
- 1 ½ tsp. apple pie spice
- ¼ cup (50g) coconut oil
- ½ cup (120ml) heavy whipping cream
- 1 cup (50g) carrots, shredded
- ½ cup (60g) walnuts, chopped

For the Instant Pot...
- 2 cups water

Method:
1. Start by greasing a 6" (15cm) cake pan that fits into your Instant Pot and setting to one side.
2. Now grab a large bowl and add all the ingredients. Blend with a hand mixer until smooth and fluffy.
3. Pour into your greased pan and cover with foil.
4. Open your Instant Pot, drop in the trivet and add the water, then lower the cake pan inside.
5. Press the cake button and cook for 40 minutes (or cook on high for 40 minutes).
6. When the timer beeps, allow the pressure to release naturally for 10 minutes, then do a quick pressure release.
7. Carefully open the lid, remove the cake and allow it to cool completely.
8. Decorate if you feel like it, serve and enjoy!

Final words...

Without meaning to sound like an infomercial, investing in an Instant Pot and getting to grips with using it really has been a life-changing experience for me. No other kitchen device has transformed the way I cook, the food choices I make and my overall health than this my Instant Pot.

And it's not just about the food- it has also allowed me to slash the time I spend in the kitchen whilst still preparing the kind of food I'm proud to serve to my family.

I hope that you will enjoy using yours too and use it to the best of your ability.

Remember, as with anything in life, there will be a learning curve and you might get confused with the buttons, and how to use the Instant Pot to the best of your cooking ability. But stick with it. You've got this thing. Just like riding a bike, you just hop right back on when you wobble, and you will soon be just fine.

So, don't just read this book, browse the recipes and then turn put away the book. Take action! Invest in an Instant Pot, borrow one from a friend or family member and then try one of the recipes in this book that you really fancy.

Who knows? You might just find yourself converted too.

Before you head into the kitchen...

Hang on! Before you dash off, let me say a quick thank you for grabbing this Book and reading your way through to the end. I hope you have fun trying the recipes I've included and even more fun eating it all. Mmmmm...

If you've enjoyed reading, please take a moment to leave me a quick review on Amazon. This tiny action on your part will help me share my recipes with the world and keep spreading the *gospel of the Instant Pot*... Or something like that.... ;)

Enjoy the book, and thank you.

Made in the USA
San Bernardino, CA
29 December 2018